BROKEN STAR—THE WARBURGS OF ALTONA

BROKEN STAR
THE WARBURGS OF ALTONA

Their Life in Germany
and
Their Death in the Holocaust

GERTRUD WENZEL

Exposition Press   Smithtown, New York

Dedicated to the members of my family
who lost their lives in persecution.

To have courage does not mean to be
without fear, but to overcome it.

ERNEST SETON THOMPSON

FIRST EDITION

© 1981 by Gertrud Wenzel

ISBN 0-682-49694-4

Printed in the United States of America

Contents

The first Warburg tombstone in Altona, in the Königstrasse cemetery:
JACOB SAMUEL WARBURG, died May 18, 1668.

Preface

It may seem strange to begin a book of memories by mentioning a tombstone. The one I mean was erected on May 18, 1668, in memory of JACOB SAMUEL WARBURG, the founder of my family. He is buried in the Königstrasse cemetery in Altona, a section of Hamburg, Germany. Albert Warburg, my grandfather, was one of his descendants in the eighth generation.

As the oldest of Albert Warburg's grandchildren, I would like to create a humble memorial for the last members of this branch of the family, because the story of my family is only one example of the lives and deaths that millions of German Jews suffered in darkest times.

The names and dates of all Warburg ancestors were written in the cemetery registers and carved on the tombstones for "time and eternity," as the saying went. The Nazis took the "eternal rest" from the Jewish cemeteries and wrote the names of those condemned to perish in the endless lists of European concentration camps. Warburgs were among the condemned.

The Warburgs had a way of ethical thought that was bred in them deeply and bound in tradition. Like millions of others, they did *not* believe that the evil long espoused in Nazi propaganda would result in vicious action—in murder. My people stayed on the Continent, although they had money in England that would have enabled them to end their lives there as free people. They were betrayed and killed.

In the German camps of mass destruction where they perished, their bodies may have turned into fertilizer, and as such they returned to German soil, to the soil of the country they had believed in. Their names have been engraved on the stone that Ernst Barlach created for the family of Albert Warburg. They had hoped to rest under this stone on the Ohlsdorf Cemetery one day. Who knows where they rest now?

In the following pages I shall try to tell you about my own family, a small group among millions of Jews who were killed in German concentration camps. Let us remember these people, who became a symbol in my mind and whose fate should rouse future generations.

1

The Ancestors

I remember my grandfather Warburg as an old gentleman. This is not astonishing, because he was sixty-three when I was born, and my memories about him begin when he was seventy.

Although he still seemed relatively young, he required help. He was looked after by a butler, and I thought it strange that *my* grandfather could not go with me on walks the way that other children's grandfathers did with them. The butler pushed my grandfather in a wheelchair through the garden. Because children have an understandable shyness about an invisible sickness, it was hard to get me to walk beside the wheelchair and talk with my grandfather about school, my friends, and "everything that interested me," as he used to say.

I preferred to sneak beside his easy chair, to the brass stand that held his newspapers and magazines, to look at pictures. There were many periodicals: *Zukunft, Simplizissimus, Jugend, Woche, Fliegende Blätter, Neue Deutsche Rundschau,* and many others, as well as daily papers in various languages and economic journals from foreign countries.

Today I can still hear the soft voice of the old gentleman saying, "That is no paper for you, my child!" And he took it from my hands.

It was a beautiful old hand, my grandfather's, which had been

1

at rest a long time, because it was no longer able to hold a pencil. Only with outstretched fingers could he hold a paper and turn a page. Often I watched this difficult action and admired it.

If I offered to help, the same remark was always the result— a remark I also often heard him make to his beloved wife: "Please no pity, my dear. We are not yet as far as that!"

Around the ring finger of his right hand there was a wedding ring in the shape of a golden rope. My grandmother wore a ring just like it, symbol of an unending tie that held the two together:

ALBERT WARBURG, *born May 23, 1843, in Altona,*
and his wife,
GERTRUDE MARGARETHA (GERTA) RINDSKOPF,
born November 23, 1856, in Amsterdam

The forefathers of the Warburg family—my grandfather was a member of the eighth generation—came from the small town of Warburg in Westphalia. About 1668, Levi Juspa—Joseph Warburg—moved to Altona, to continue his money-exchange business there. (At that period every German state had its own money, so a lot of exchanging had to be done.) He died between 1676 and 1680.

The following dates have been taken from documents and from the tomb inscriptions in the Jewish cemeteries of Königstrasse and Breitestrasse in Altona. The facts were collected before the First World War.

The name of the forefather of all Altona Warburgs, Joseph Warburg, was inscribed on the tombstone of his son, Jacob Samuel Warburg. A photograph of this stone is shown in this book. This son died on May 18, 1668, and is buried in Königstrasse. The tomb carries the number 1162.

Jacob Samuel Warburg was a businessman in the Altona Jewish community. The epitaph describes him as an "honest and faithful man." He was married to Reizche, daughter of the learned president of the community, Samson Ruben Goldzieher.

She died on August 25, 1674. They had four sons: Moses, Samson, Seligman, and Ruben.

Moses Samuel Warburg, businessman and scholar, continued the line of our Warburgs. He died on May 28, 1701, and rests under tombstone 1212 in Königstrasse. From his marriage with Hitzia (Hintual), daughter of Meier Heilbut, who died on February 17, 1693, came Samuel Warburg.

Samuel Warburg was also called Frankfurter, probably because he studied in Frankfurt. He died on April 18, 1759, and rests in grave 1735, Königstrasse. His wife, Zippora Rachel, was the daughter of the president of the Jewish community in Hamburg, Elias Wiener, called Meschulim Delbanco. Zippora died on August 23, 1783. The couple had five sons: Moses, Elias, Gumprich-Moses, Simon (–Simia) and Ascher-Amschel.

Moses Warburg, called Frankfurter, died while his father was still alive, on January 24, 1753, and rests under stone 3482 in Königstrasse. His wife, Elkel (Ella), died on Monday, May 11, 1758, as can be read from the funeral records in Altona.

Their son, Salomon Moses Warburg, called Frankfurter, was born on August 17, 1747, and died on April 2, 1824. His grave is number 2795 in the Königstrasse cemetery. He was a cashier in the Jewish community in Altona and the founder of the S. Warburg banking establishment. In the Altona directory for 1791 the business of Salomon Warburg, Breitestrasse 298, was called a "money exchange and paper shop." He married Zippora, daughter of the honorary taxation commissioner Moses Leidersdorff. She died on June 2, 1796, and lies next to her husband in grave 2794. They had three sons: Wolff Salomon, Samuel Salomon, and Menschem-Mendel, called Martin-Salomon.

Wolff Salomon Warburg, born on November 9, 1778, first became a teacher. In 1806 he entered the banking business that his father had founded, and on January 23, 1805, he married Bela Betty, daughter of Levin Lazarus Stieber, president of the Hamburg Jewish community.

For decades Wolff S. Warburg was president of the Altona Jewish community. Without making conditions he gave a great

SALOMON WARBURG, founder of the Altona Bank, about 1825

deal of money to his wife, Betty Warburg, "to do charity to her heart's content," as the documents report. Wolff S. Warburg died on January 3, 1854. The dates of his wife are October 5, 1782, to April 13, 1862. The couple lie in graves 1449 and 1450 in the Königstrasse cemetery. The Hebrew inscriptions on the rear of their tombstones may be translated as follows:

> *From all the rich and fruitful days*
> *Your road to peace eternal led.*
> *Accomplished is your earthly work*
> *so deep, devout and noble.*
> *Though the body be dust, the spirit lives on*
> *in all the seed you have scattered.*
> *Skyward the sublime shoots are soaring.*
> *No death can ever destroy them.*

The following poem is for his wife, Betty Warburg:

> *To Heaven your faith was given.*
> *Ever true you were to your God.*
> *Your only desire down on this earth*
> *was to do good as Love demands.*
> *Now your heart so warm and your mind so quick*
> *have gone to their eternal rest,*
> *and orphaned now are those you loved.*

Wolff S. and Betty Warburg had four sons. The oldest, Lesser, was born on March 24, 1807. He was a printer and died unmarried on August 18, 1851, in Schleswig-Holstein. Moses, the second son, was called Moritz. He was born on June 28, 1810, a silent partner in the W. S. Warburg banking business. He was my great-grandfather.

The next son, John, was born in 1812 and died in 1886. He married Laura Stettiner. She was born in 1839 and died in 1881. They had no children. John was a partner in the W. S. Warburg bank, as was the last son, Pius, who was born in 1816.

Pius Warburg was a member of the Altona city council, and from 1871 to 1887 he served on the Provincial Committee.

In memory of his mother, Betty, he established the Betty Foundation. According to the 1916 papers this was a foundation for "unmarried females without special profession or status."

From a letter that a member of the executive committee wrote me in 1967, I note that the rules and regulations of the Betty Foundation have adjusted the rights and obligations of its members to meet modern conditions. No statement of need is required.

In 1967 there was a monthly housing allotment of ten Deutschmarks. The foundation helps old people find a place to live. Seventy-six people of both sexes now live in the available rooms, but the foundation plans to devote its activities primarily to single women. The letter concluded: "And finally let us not forget our garden. The fruit trees are so numerous that we always can distribute many apples and pears to our old people—free of charge, of course!"

I have already mentioned that Moritz Warburg, my great-grandfather, was born on June 28, 1810. A lawyer, he had the title of Dr. Juris. (doctor of laws). He was a solicitor and notary in Altona. From 1848 to 1850 he represented his home town in the Schleswig-Holstein legislature, and from 1867 to 1886 he was a member of the Prussian House of Deputies. He died in 1886 and is buried in the Bornekampsweg cemetery.

Moritz Warburg was married to Helene Cohen, a native of Hannover. Her family were descendants of Leffmann Behrens Cohen, and had lived in Hannover for eight generations. Nathan Spanier also belongs to this old Altona family circle. In 1612 he obtained the right to settle there from the Count of Schauenburg and in the end became superintendent of Schauenburg Province.

Dr. Jur. Moritz Warburg and his wife, Helene Cohen, had five children: Sophie, Albert, Charlotte, Jacob, and Siegfried. Their second child and eldest son, Albert, was my grandfather.

Albert Warburg was born on June 23, 1843, in Altona, and died on February 19, 1919, in Hamburg. He was manager of the W. S. Warburg bank in Altona and for many years was deputy chairman of the chamber of commerce of his home town. The distinction of the title "Geheimer Kommerzienrat" meant very little to the quiet and humble businessman, just as little as decorations and other honors.

One day I was walking beside my grandfather, who was in his wheelchair. I knew that he would have loved to hold my hand while we went along. But his hands lay motionless and waxen on his knees. His hands did not even seem to belong to him.

"You know, Gertrud," he said, "I was always especially interested in school problems, because I have never been in a school. In my time children like us were taught by a tutor, who also had to look after our general education. That was not as nice as your school at all. You have to go there, but you can make lifelong friends, and you can come home with a report card."

"That sounds terribly sad, grandfather," I said. "Wasn't your school at home fun? I think it would be wonderful not to have a long way to go to school in wet weather, for example, and not to be afraid to come home with a bad report card! I expect that your tutor told your parents at once when your efforts were not satisfactory?"

"Yes, that was so. We also did not have so many hours of teaching as you have now. Instead we had to read ever so much more! The tutor lived in our home, and we often shared some meals. No, that's not right. It was different. At eight A.M. we began our schoolwork sitting at a long table, with the tutor at the end of it. Then at eleven he ordered another meal for himself. The old butler, Jacob, who seemed to have been in the house forever, then brought a tray with delicious food. There was coffee. Its aroma crept right up our noses. We could see appetizing small sandwiches, and a beautiful bowl with tasty fruit. But for us students there only was a plate with a dry slice of bread each. We then had to eat without looking greedily at our tutor's meal. How we hoped that something tasty might be left over for us! If that exercise worked out satisfactorily, our tutor was very happy indeed! And you, my dear, would *you* like this method of education?"

I did not think it was worthwhile at all! I thought it was something like cruelty to animals. But whether I told grandfather so I do not remember.

The past of which Grandfather Warburg spoke I met— though not in words—once a week in Flottbeck. The large gong at the back entrance was rung in a special rhythm when grandfather was in the garden. This meant the family doctor had arrived. The old Dr. med. Nap Trier, whose father, Napoleon, had tended the older generation of Warburgs, had driven up from the main road in his carriage and was one of the people who were permitted to ring the front door bell.

How well I knew the noise that the hooves of the old mare made when they stopped at the entrance! I hurried into the hall to be there when the maid opened the door for the old doctor. There I stood—hands at my back, I am still certain of it—to see what was going on. First Nap Trier took off his old black coat. The velvet collar was always slightly dusty. Then he took his top hat off. And to my greatest fascination there was something under this. It looked like a flat silk hat without a rim. I thought this was really interesting, and I was always waiting for the day, when for once there would not be a second hat!

The father of old Nap Trier, whose name was a sign of his great admiration for the Emperor Napoleon, tended daily to the old "uncles." He asked about their various aches and pains in the same way that a grocer asks about something missing on the kitchen shelf.

The uncles lived in the house at Palmaille No. 31. They were the brothers Pius, John, and Moritz Warburg. Many charming stories were told about them. One of the trio, it was said, always carried a small piece of chalk in the pockets of his beautiful velvet waistcoat. He changed his waistcoat every day. And if he had some pains somewhere, he drew a small chalk cross on the vest at the spot where it hurt. And when Napoleon

Trier came the next day—one could only say to see his customers
—the uncle would say to the butler Jacob, "Jacob, get me the
waistcoat from yesterday. I want to show our doctor where I
had such miserable pains yesterday!"

The old Warburg uncles were very well known in Altona.
There's a story that a smart-alecky young nephew, who studied
in Rome, addressed a postcard as follows: "Uncle Pius, Altona."
And the card arrived!

The old uncles were portrayed very realistically by their
friend the painter Christian Wilhelm Allers (1857-1915). In the
picture they were playing whist: smoking their cigars, con-
centrating on their game. A good sense of humor shone in the
corners of their eyes. For young people of their time, they could
not be overlooked; they formed a real clique, because they were
very close. My grandmother Warburg told me several times that,
in 1876, when she got married at nineteen, those three old
gentlemen were very, very old. She said their total age was over
two hundred!

There she was, young Gerta, as she was called, in a foreign
country, in a foreign city, with nobody but old people. But the
three old gentlemen took care of her very enthusiastically. Their
gallantry enchanted her. Because of her charm, vivacity and
intelligence, Gerta Warburg was soon their favorite family
member.

The family of Gertrude Margaretha (Gerta) Warburg, nee
Rindskopf, can be traced back to the end of the eighteenth century,
to the Cahn family of Bonn. Let us begin with Jonas Cahn. He
was born on December 4, 1792, and died on July 23, 1856.
His wife was Gertrude Beckard, who came from Kreuznach. We
know only the date of her death, January 17, 1850. The couple
had thirteen children. Their names reflect the time of the French
occupation as well as German patriotism and the parents' Jewish
tradition: Hermann, Abraham/Albert, Regina, Jeanette, Jonas,

GERTA WARBURG, about 1880

Julie, Friedrich, Hugo, David, Helene, Odilie, Friedrich August, and Pauline.

The sisters Julie and Helene Cahn from Bonn married the brothers Leopold and Julius Rindskopf from Frankfurt. As young married couples the brothers Rindskopf emigrated with the Cahn sisters from Frankfurt to Amsterdam. Here are their dates:

JULIUS RINDSKOPF:

>born April 10, 1817, in Frankfurt
>died April 10, 1875, in Amsterdam

>and his wife

HELENE CAHN:

>born July 31, 1832, in Bonn
>died November 22, 1865, in Amsterdam

They had six children: Alice Mathilde, Gertrude Margaretha, Catherine Susanne, Emil Jonas—who died at the age of thirteen —and the twins Marie and Paula. (Marie died when she was twenty-four.)

When my grandmother Gertrude Margaretha was only eight, she lost her mother, and when she was eighteen her father died. Because he had wanted his children to stay in their parental home on the Keizersgracht in Amsterdam, their uncle Leopold Rindskopf and his wife, Julie, moved into the large house and brought their three children, Martin Josef, Theodor Jonas and Anna Gertrude, with them.

The extremely ambitious and austere "Aunt Julie," as my grandmother called her, managed, in years to come, to get the daughters of her late sister married back to Germany. Their husbands were well-known bank managers with sizable fortunes. Only Gertrude Margaretha refused to marry a gentleman selected by her aunt. During a visit to another aunt in Plittersdorf on the Rhine, she chose her husband herself, as she often very proudly stressed. That she and her later spouse had both been invited for a stay in the roomy house on the Rhine, to meet each other, she certainly would *not* have liked to hear.

Albert Warburg and Gertrude Margaretha (Gerta) Rindskopf

were married on November 16, 1876. The young couple lived in a small house near the railway station in Altona. My grandmother and I often walked past the house when we went to town. An old grapevine climbed to the first floor. It wove a pretty wreath around a small balcony, which was adorned by a wrought-iron railing.

2

The Palmaille

The house at Palmaille No. 31, often mentioned in these pages, was owned by grandfather's younger brother, the Counselor of Justice and notary Dr. Siegfried Warburg, and his large family. I often visited the old gentleman, holding my grandmother's or mother's hand tightly. I would have been too frightened to go alone. The hall and staircase were strangely dark, and only a little light came in from a large skylight. This was the building style of that period. The statue of a scantily clad female who held three torches resembling lamps, lit by gas, did not do much to illuminate the hall.

This beautiful old home was built on a very large piece of land. Soon the small house near the railway station, where my grandparents had begun their married life, became too small for their growing family and the increasing social and business obligations of a well-known banker. Therefore, Albert Warburg asked the famous architect Manfred Semper to build him a suitable house on the family ground. This became No. 33.

We often asked grandmother about the meaning of "Palmaille," which was not followed by a word like "road," "path," "way," or "avenue." She took us into grandfather's library on the first floor of the house, opened a window, and made us look left and right along the street. Leaning out a bit, we could see far on both sides. Grandmother then closed the window and told us that, at the end of the seventeenth century, the last Count of Schauenburg, Otto VI, had ordered his gardeners to plant several straight lines of trees. In the shade of these trees the Count and his visitors intended to play an Italian game that had just become fashionable. As in croquet, a ball had to be driven through wire arches with a long-handled mallet. At the court of Louis XIV the game was called pall-mall, from the Italian *pallomaglio*. German slang changed it to "Palmaille."

In my grandparents' day, the game was long forgotten, and it is very doubtful that anybody in Altona had any idea of where the name of their most beautiful street had come from. Old burgher houses, which displayed their owners' wealth, lined the Palmaille and gave it a feudal aspect. Traffic never disturbed the tree-lined avenue, and neither the horse trolley nor later electric trolleys were permitted to shatter the harmony of this elegant street.

During the Second World War, Allied bombs erased both Warburg houses from the Palmaille, from Altona, and from the world. In postwar urban planning, everything was changed. The atmosphere of the old Palmaille and of the old Warburgs who had lived there was destroyed forever.

"*The* Palmaille," as the house at No. 33 was called by relatives and friends, was a city mansion. During the winter months my grandmother saw to it that life went according to French etiquette. Not only the parties, which brought the elegant society to her house, but the "*jour fixe*" she had every week gave the city a cosmopolitan air. One day every week the Palmaille opened its doors to everything that was beautiful and interesting. Old friends introduced their aquaintances of name and social position; young friends brought their gifted colleagues. People met each other, chatted, discussed, understood each other, learned to esteem one another, and came again. New visitors constantly joined the circle, and the most various ties were formed from these meetings.

The nearly circular drawing room on the ground floor, dedicated to musical evenings only, featured an excellent Steinway grand piano. Johannes Brahms and Pius Warburg, who unpretentiously composed music under the pseudonym Paul Werner, used the instrument during the soirees. These evenings in the Palmaille attracted musically inclined guests, to the delight of Gerta Warburg, lady of the house. Her only sorrow was that none of her three daughters was musical at all.

But my grandmother's love, her intense interest, belonged to the visual arts. From a home filled with sentiment for all that was beautiful, having grown up in close contact with all the Dutch museums, with their treasures of Italian and French paintings, she returned from journeys to gray Holland. She knew the splendors of most European museums and brought this deeply rooted knowledge into her marriage. Exceptionally well read and gifted with an excellent memory, she was destined to be a wife with bel esprit and sparkling wit, married to a far-seeing businessman, my grandfather Warburg.

With her great knowledge and exquisite taste, she tried to help contemporary artists. The biblical way of "Never let the left hand know what the right hand does" meant here that the Warburgs represented the two hands. Some of the artists whom my grandmother fostered have long since joined the ranks of the immortals.

For some years after the house at Palmaille No. 33 was finished, a painting for the hall on the first floor was needed. It certainly was courageous in that period for my grandmother to ask a foreign artist, hardly known in Germany at all, to paint a portrait of her eldest daughter. The artist was the Norwegian Edvard Munch, now considered one of the greatest modern painters. Today the portrait hangs in the Kunsthaus Zürich, witness of another time and another world.

Grandmother was also extremely interested, as she said herself, in the works of Ernst Barlach. I can still remember a trip with grandmother to Güstrow. We went to visit Barlach in his studio. She and the artist talked on and on. The child Gertrud was terribly bored at walking around between huge blocks of wood. Grandmother often leafed through the large etchings. I remember the first print of Barlach's *Der tote Tag*.

Barlach gave it to grandmother. It disappeared in Holland in 1940. Only the large tombstone that Barlach created for the Warburgs stands as testimonial to the spiritual tie between them.

The indoor life at Palmaille No. 33 was always stimulating. Rarely did the family go into the garden, but there was a view of the Elbe River, the wharves, and in the far distance the green pasture land. Incoming and outgoing ocean liners wove a connection with distant parts of the world, for which the garden was merely a teeny-tiny spot on the round globe. Only trees, shrubs, and lawns connected the houses at Palmaille Nos. 33 and 31. At the end was a pavilion, where occasionally family gatherings took place and from where we saw the big ships sailing out.

But how can I give my contemporaries and their descendants —if they are interested at all—any idea of such a way of life, so very different from our technical and purpose-centered time? Do the rooms at Palmaille No. 33, their size and number, signify anything? Hardly. Does it matter that the house had three floors and a fully used basement? No. Is anybody impressed because the drawing room to the garden could be opened to a ballroom where a hundred guests could sit? Certainly not. Does the number of "servants" mean anything: a coachman, a butler, a chambermaid, a housemaid, a female cook, and her young help, a laundress, and an ironing woman? No. But in the end all these details weave a pattern of what it meant to have a manorial household before the First World War.

I recall the long dining room with its high window opening to the Palmaille. Portraits by various old Dutch masters hung on the dark paneled walls. Grandmother had brought them from her home in Amsterdam. What strict-looking gentlemen, wearing "millstone collars," and ladies with frocks buttoned up to their chin! The wives were painted by Victor Bol, Johannes Victors, Johannes Cornelis Verspronck, and others. I loved to sit at table opposite a family group portrait by Thomas de Keyser, which showed the extremely puritan-looking parents sitting in the garden, and their young, slim, and pretty daughter standing in the background. I wondered whom the pretty girl resembled more, father or mother. I could not decide. I also liked the portrait of a lady by van den Tempel. She wore a wide lace collar, and the fan she held was extremely fascinating to me.

Some of these serene Dutchmen had their hands resting on dark chairs, covered with black leather, which was fastened to the wood of the chair by heavy-headed brass nails. Grandfather Warburg had these painted chairs copied for his dining room, and once, when I was still very young, he said to me, "Look, Gertrud, how strong the old gentleman in that picture still is! He lifted one of our chairs up to the painting! Watch him, he will sit down up there in a moment!"

There were numerous pieces of Dutch pottery on the mantelpiece and around the dining room. I was not interested in them, but two cows I thought fascinating: their mouths were bright blue, they had yellow udders, and they were decorated all over with colorful stylized flowers. I could not get used to these unusual animals and asked grandmother why they looked so strange.

"You see, Gertrud, the cows have devoured so many flowers in good Dutch meadows that the flowers grew through their skins!"

These two cows, which had already lost one ear each, were given to me by my grandmother. They stood on the mantelpiece of my Gruiten house, and my children asked why there were flowers all over them. I handed on the explanation that grandmother gave me, but here also doubt and criticism predominated. And if the whole world does not fall to pieces, my grandchildren will ask the same question, and I hope that these two Delft cows may impress a few more generations!

The butler served the meals in the dark dining room. He stood close to a food elevator, which transported the dishes from the kitchen in the basement to any floor where the food was wanted. His hands in white gloves at his back, the butler waited. He always waited: for the food to come up, for a sign from the master of the house to pour out wine, for a sign from the lady of the house to take dishes away, for a timid sign from us children to give us a helping hand when our stiffly starched napkins had slid to the floor. And when the butler had to answer a question, he whispered. He was the most perfect and admirable figure in the house.

When my mother was permitted to participate in a big formal dinner for the first time, she got a frock with a low-cut neckline for the occasion. The old butler, observing her coming downstairs, very slowly and proud, was upset and whispered, "Miss Ellen, excuse me, but you forgot to put on your frock."

My grandparents had three good-looking daughters. Helene Julie, called Ellen, was born in 1877; she became my mother. Next came Ada Sophie, born in 1878, and in 1881 Betty. Their only son, Wilhelm, born in 1884, died when Altona was struck by a diptheria epidemic. He was only seven years old.

The education of the daughters was meant to meet the demands made on girls from the "best" society. Because schools did not have high standards, tutors widened the general horizon. English and French governesses saw to it that the girls got the best foreign language instruction, and the artistic inclinations of the young ladies were fostered by well-known artists. But it was their very strict mother who gave them their final polish in behavior and manners.

It is said that grandmother, who had a certain code word regarding manners at table, was not happy about one of her daughters leaning in her chair. The girl was probably absorbed in a conversation with the person next to her. Grandmother called "Swan!" This meant: "Sit straight!" The young lady did not alter her position until she heard her mother call in a loud voice "Swaner!"

Soirees, dinners, and dances were great Altona social events at Palmaille No. 33. The young officers of the garrison, as well as the assistants at law, were happy to be honored with invitations. Everybody knew that everything offered *Chez Warburg* would be of the highest style and taste. Often the Hamburg painter Thomas Herbst—a friend of the hostess—painted the design for the invitation cards, which the three daughters Warburg then elaborated with gracious watercolors. According to house rules, these cards had to be shown at the entrance of the Palmaille, to keep strangers out.

Grandfather Warburg often played a prank. He would stand at the door, dressed in a magnificent livery with numerous gold buttons, braids, a curly wig, and old-fashioned spectacles. To the astonishment and amusement of his visitors, he sometimes addressed them by their nicknames. How he enjoyed his jokes!

Dr. iur. Edgar Burchard was also once invited for a festive dance in my grandparents' house. The story has it that he fell in love with Ellen Warburg, the eldest daughter, during their first waltz. Just what conversation the young gentleman used to enchant the lady of his heart is far from a daughter's knowledge. Dr. Burchard was always said to be an entertainer with a good sense of humor and very chivalrous. It was the time of light and whimsical conversation:

"I am very keen to know, beautiful lady, if you would like to be a swan?"

"Oh, no, sir, what an idea! All day with the belly on cold water!"

Ellen Warburg probably told her mother all about this young solicitor. Amusing people could always count on grandmother's sympathy! Soon the young gentleman was invited to dinners in the private family circle, and he presented himself as well as possible. A young lover gets to his goal fastest by courting his future mother-in-law, and Dr. Burchard won grandmother's heart *very* fast, because of his charm and his sense of humor. The excellent understanding between them deepened more and more the longer they knew each other.

But, even so, it was hard for the grandparents Warburg to give their eldest daughter away to a gentleman from Breslau who was two years her junior. Perhaps they were hoping for a respectable Hamburg businessman. But the information that my grandfather as banker obtained about his future son-in-law was so good that nothing could prevent the engagement. The contribution that the eye specialist Dr. med. Albert Burchard added to the household money of his son, who had not yet finished his legal studies, and the pin money that the counselor Warburg gave his daughter, enabled the young couple to start their own household.

To avoid difficulties in the education of possible offspring, the strictly Puritan father Burchard demanded that Ellen Warburg be converted to Protestantism. Because of the freedom of thought always practiced in the Warburgs' Jewish home, there was no objection to this demand. Ellen Warburg was baptized on May 12, 1905, in the St. Katharinen Church in Hamburg, by the minister, Dr. Stage.

Photographs from the time of my parents' engagement show my quiet mother with a rather timid expression. (Father may have been too ardent a lover!) Dressed in a tight-fitting white moreen silk frock, a wreath of orange blossoms in her hair and with an enormous bouquet of orchids, Ellen Warburg in her beauty was regal, charming and graceful.

When Dr. Jur. Edgar Eduard Walter Burchard from Breslau and Helene Julie (Ellen) Warburg from Altona were married on May 25, 1905, in the St. Katharinen Church in Hamburg, Dr. Stage celebrated the occasion. Later, he performed still another Protestant ceremony: *my* baptism. True to the legal correctness of the young husband and the inherited businesslike precision of the young wife, I, Gertrud, arrived after nine months, as the eldest of four Burchard offspring, in March 1906, followed by Albert, Oswald, and Marie at wholesome two-year intervals.

After the marriage of their eldest daughter, the social life at the Palmaille continued. The story has it that one afternoon, following a festive evening, some unpopular nieces dropped in for a cup of tea and gossip about the guests of the previous evening.

One of these girls remarked critically, "Miss X. looked rather beautiful last night—but she had such heavy makeup!"

"You may paint yourself too, if you think it would improve your looks!" said grandmother, who had listened to the conversation from her room next door. She had never used powder or perfume, but pardoned *"corriger la fortune"* for anybody she thought needed it!

She had her own approach to beauty, but never lost her sense of realism. She once demonstrated this in Rome, where we had a wonderful time together. My brother Albert and I, then in our teens, stood behind a group of American tourists and tried to see the whole statue of the famous Apollo Belvedere. It was hardly possible in the crowd. My brother asked whether the god had full human size. The old lady pulled her handkerchief from her pocket, measured her grandson's leg from knee to ankle, held the measurement between her fingers, and elbowed her way through the crowd to get to the statue of the god. There she measured the same part of the leg, comparing it with Albert's measurements, and stated with raised voice that the famous statue was *under* life-size!

"Gertrud, don't look at him anymore! He is as beautiful as an undressed lieutenant of the reserves! Always remember, good-looking men are not worth much!"

She had her aversions, my beloved grandmother, whom I loved to call "Olli" when I was a child. But some old aunts, spinsterish and rather bourgeois, did not think this name honorable enough. In the end I had the idea of calling the old lady *"Granny,"* a name we both liked very much. All the time that we both wandered over the crust of this restless earth, we stuck to the name, and grandmother signed her numerous letters to me with "Granny," or with only a lofty *"G."*

Strangely enough, Granny also had a strict aversion against jewelry, although she owned beautiful old pieces from her mother and pretty ones that grandfather had given her when they were young. After a German caricaturist had painted bankers' wives covered with diamonds, glittering like stars, she locked all her jewelry in a safe and never wore it again. She used only her pearl earrings and a few simple brooches, and her wedding ring, which she may have worn when she perished.

If some visitor in the Palmaille wanted to honor her by wearing a lot of jewelry, she could say in an amiably spiteful way, "My dear, it is really not necessary to come to see me looking like an open safe! You really exaggerate, dearest. After all, you do not intend to look like an aborigine, do you?"

Just as she was not impressed by jewelry, money was not for showing off. Certainly, money was necessary to live, but there was never any talk about it in my grandparents' house. If visitors started telling the prices of goods, or their financial value, Granny cut off the subject with the well-known remark: "One does not talk about money; one *has* it!"

As I was told, this statement was never meant snobbishly. It was one of Granny's quotations, which also was heard in other Hamburg families. I wonder who said it first.

But Granny tidily noted all the expenses of her large household in a huge notebook with numerous columns, which grandfather checked from time to time. If the expenses did not tally with the household money left, Granny would note graciously: "Haberdashery—Mark 100" (about $25)—a huge amount, for which one could have bought a whole shop full of needles, thread, elastics, and buttons at the beginning of this century!

The writing table, on which these keen financial manipulations were done, stood before the window of the large family drawing room on the first floor of the house at Palmaille No. 33. From her easy chair, looking up, Granny could enjoy the magnificent view over the Elbe. The seat at the window was really her very own place in the house. The little sewing table with inlay work was one of the most fascinating pieces of furniture during my childhood. The lid could be lifted and fixed at a certain angle, and in this way it was changed into a dressing table with a mirror inside. When it was open, many small divisions, each with a specially inlaid decorated cover, could be seen. How often I sat on a footstool at Granny's feet, watching her alter a new, modish, and extremely expensive hat! She took it all to pieces. Flowers, feathers, veils, and ribbons were gathered on her lap. Later she sewed it all back to the hat, slightly different from the milliner's ideas, of course, but to her way of taste and thought it was *much* more elegant than before!

Then the hat had to be "aired."

"Come, Gertrud, let us have a walk to one of the cemeteries. We will be quite alone there. Wouldn't that be nice?"

I agreed to every suggestion, as long as I was alone with my beloved Granny. So we walked hand in hand to the Jewish cemetery, where she explained the shapes of the various tombstones. These instructions fascinated me much less than the robin's nest in one of the many dense hedges. One walk with

Granny was just as wonderful as another, regardless of where we went: passing the theater, along to the station, where I had to listen to the story of the first trains, or when we stopped before the monument to the old Kaiser, where I heard a history lesson. She always made me see things with her own eyes.

This time, for a change, we went to a Jewish cemetery. There were never any conversations about religion or creeds in the Palmaille. There was also never any questioning of a person's creed; they were all Protestant in Altona anyhow, and in all of Hamburg too. I never heard the words "Jew," "Jewish, or "Judaism" in my youth. I am quite certain that, if I had, I would have inquired about their meaning, in normal juvenile inquisitiveness, especially because our questions were never waved away with the easygoing "You don't understand this, my child!" or "For this problem you are still much too young!"

If we wanted to, we could inform ourselves about many things on our own. On Sundays we were permitted to get the large Bible volumes off the shelves. We adored looking at the famous Gustave Doré illustrations, leaf after leaf, while Granny told us the corresponding tales. I shall never forget the last picture of the Deluge: one tip of a rock still rises out of the tremendous sheet of water, and close together drowning humans cling to it. Perched high on the stone is a tigress, holding her cub up to safety. A naked human mother, a baby in her arms, tries to climb, battling for this highest spot. How tremendously exciting it all was! We carefully considered their chances, and our trembling hearts came to the conclusion that the human mother *had* to lose when the tigress hit her with her claws! It was unimaginable!

We suffered with Hagar and Ishmael in the desert. Nothing could give us children any hope for the solution of their hunger and thirst problems. All we saw was an empty, turned-over waterjug.

Granny answered our dense questions laconically: "Help will be given."

Did the words "God" or "Lord" come up? They did not.

And so the figures in the Old and New Testaments were well known to us. To us David was a hero after his victorious battle with Goliath, a hero like those in other stories: the Trojan Horse, the Golden Fleece, the Nibelungs. We studied the illustrations in the Bibles intensely, and no remark from Granny's side ever troubled our enthusiasm.

Understandably, after the first volume, called "Old Testament," the second, "New Testament," followed. It was much thinner than the other. We knew the stories better from our governesses. We preferred the pictures in it to those of the Old Testament, because Jesus was such a good-looking man and we could admire so many halos. And when there was something as distressing as the numerous cripples and sick people, He could help. We thought it all wonderful and very understandable. So we did not ask Granny for explanations, which probably pleased her. To her the words of Frederick II meant most: "In this country, everybody may find his salvation in his own way!"

Looking at illustrated books was the most wonderful thing to us in the Palmaille! Granny placed large volumes on a couch under the window. We pulled footstools close to it and admired the pictures in enormous blue tomes, called "Museum," where all works of art displayed in European museums could be seen. We had to look at all of them; there was no choosing. Also, we were not meant to look at the pictures only; we also had to memorize the names of the artists. Suddenly Granny would stand behind us, covering the print under the illustration with her hand. *Who painted the portrait?* Depending on our answers her expression would vary from hearty pleasure to great disappointment. After all, our ages at that time ranged between five and eleven years!

A large part of the drawing room was taken up by a semicircular settee in a corner. Over it a similar-shaped ebony shelf displayed the exotic pieces so fashionable at that time. All in the best style and quality.

There was a bronze Buddha with an enormous belly and legs. While I looked at him, kneeling on the settee, Granny asked my father, "Edgar, would you be so kind and explain to Gertrud the meaning of Buddha's way of holding his hand?

Father was unable to oblige; he was interested in other things. Charmingly he kissed Granny's hand. She seemed very pleased, and that was the end of the Buddha problem.

Beside him, as an Oriental neighbor, there was a Siva with numerous arms. As I was busily studying all these strange figures, I asked father, who stood behind me, why this odd dancer had so many arms.

"Well, Tutti, I can answer your question only in my own way, though I do not know whether Granny thinks the same: Imagine what a wonderful show this god would put on in an apple-picking contest! He would fill his basket in a whiz!"

Granny played dumb and seemed not to have heard father's answer. I turned toward the Sleeping Lion from Lucerne. I thought him so boring that I did not ask any question. But my brother Albert, who for some time had been kneeling beside me on the settee, turned to Granny with a question regarding "Ariadne on Naxos": "Would Naxos bite me?"

A quiet shaking of Granny's head showed Albert that his question was silly. Obviously a lot was still missing in the general field called "education." I did not mix in, though I had learned already that Naxos was not the name of the lion Ariadne was riding on, but of the Greek island where it all took place!

Every morning Granny was enthroned in a corner of that settee when she discussed the daily menu with the cook. The lady of the house listened carefully to all suggestions given by the kitchen chief, but in the end it was Granny who ruled with dignity and perserverance.

In her time the servants in Hamburg (and Altona) received weekly "donations" stipulated in special regulations. At the beginning of our century there were, among other goods, 1 pound butter, 2 pounds sugar, and 1 pound coffee beans. They could do what they wanted with these legal donations: eat them or sell them, give them to friends or relatives; they were just their own. The servants' regulations also stated that the domestics could object to more than two meals of salmon per week.

At that period, salmon was the most plentiful and inexpensive Elbe fish.

I expect that Granny felt as safe as in a fortress when she was perched in her settee corner. From there she negotiated not only with her own servants, but also with tradesmen, tailors, dressmakers, milliners, and last but not least with her grandchildren.

There were still other items on the shelf behind her. There was a round, black enamel box, the lid decorated with a landscape from gleaming mother-of-pearl work, showing Chinese pagodas in the background, nearly hidden by some bamboo and, in the foreground, a dainty little bridge, which led over water to a tiny island. It was within easy reach. To stare at it was strictly forbidden! This box contained chocolates for children: flat round "coins" covered with tiny colorful sugar beads— rewards. To stare at the handsome box seemed like a demand for a chocolate, Granny thought, and that was bad manners!

Knowing that it would give her much pleasure, we recited long classical poems, possibly with vast and impressive gestures, and if necessary with trembling voices—and we were certain to get a chocolate. Granny's way of looking at us was a touching mixture of pride and admiration. Today I am still ashamed of myself for having greedily stretched out my hand at once after finishing a long ballad, to get my sweet reward.

But there was still another box for chocolates on the shelf, of Japanese cloisonné. These were sweets for adults, and they were bought by Granny herself in a small shop on Altona's Breitestrasse. There, old Miss Müller stood in her small store. She had three samples of her goods displayed on tiny flat glass plates, while the same delicacies stood stacked by the pound in colorful tins on various shelves.

Granny and I walked from the Palmaille to the Breitestrasse. She held my hand and I could feel her warmth through the thin kid glove. That was unbelievably wonderful for me! Wearing a tight-fitting black tailor-made costume, a smart little hat with a veil, and made-to-measure button-up booties (which her chambermaid had to break in when they were new), my grandmother seemed to me the perfection of simple elegance.

Shopping at Miss Müller's was always the same, and very quick indeed:

"The same as usual, please, Miss Müller, I take the parcel along with me!" was all Granny had to say.

The old saleswoman, her hair divided in the center of her head and taken to the side in equal waves, decorated herself— after having smilingly heard and accepted the order—with a pair of tiny golden spectacles, armed herself with a kind of sugar tongs, got four of the promising-looking tins from the shelves, and began her job. First she grabbed a flat-folded pink paper bag, which she got into the desired shape by gliding her small hand into it. Hands behind my back, I followed all the procedures every time with due excitement and feverish attention, knowing that in the end there would be something for me too.

Miss Müller's small hand went with fast, angular movements with the tong into the tins, taking out one sweetmeat at a time. It fell into the paper bag with a tiny noise I thought tremendously exciting. The mixture was even and no kind got a preference. The pink bag was then placed on the brass scales, as brightly polished as the weighing stones. The weight was at once perfectly exact, nothing had to be added, and a sigh of relief finished the weighing scene. Miss Müller's pale cheeks got red spots from the hard work, and she almost looked pretty.

The pink paper bag was folded elaborately at the top rim, tied with a pretty blue ribbon, which she knotted carefully, and a bow was added. Meanwhile, Granny had taken a silver purse from the pocket of her jacket and paid with shiny new coins, which grandfather had brought from his bank to pay her household bills. The way Granny handled these coins, how she made them slide onto the counter, made her look absolutely royal in my eyes.

And then the miracle occurred: the sweet-tongs dived once more into one of the tins, the contents of which I did not know. Miss Müller tripped around the counter and put a piece of chocolate on my flat outstretched hand, which still had the woolen glove on. Then she shyly enjoyed my great delight, her hands folded behind her back.

Granny had already taken the pink paper bag, because she knew the coming procedure in advance. She hung the bag by the loop over her middle finger, and nodded amiably toward Miss Müller, who held the door open for us. The businesswoman may have followed us for a while with her eyes. Only after some time did I hear the music that some bells created at the closing of the door.

Once it happened that the sweets for adults were so much liked by one of the maids that Granny saw the chocolate level fall rapidly, without knowing who had enjoyed the contents of the blue box. So she ordered the same sweetmeats from Miss Müller, but filled with castor oil. The pale chambermaid, who dusted the shelf over the settee the next morning, from time to time holding her hurting belly, did not get a harsh word from Granny, who sat in her easy chair, looking through the mail. For her all was now again settled for good. And so it was.

We grandchildren liked the coachman, John, best. Without moving at all, he sat on his coachbox, wearing a top hat and a huge bearskin collar, and waited for grandfather, whom twice a day he took to the bank. When snow fell, it accumulated on the top hat, enlarging it rather impressively, and in John's beard we could see glittering drops.

Only when I was grown-up myself could I understand Granny's expression "Good servants have no sex!" In her way of thinking, this meant that one should never appear before a visitor in a dressing gown, but it did not matter at all if the butler of the house saw you in this attire!

The last butler of a long line was a man who called himself Simon Bad. My father disliked him at once. He looked after grandfather very well, spoke five languages fluently, and had other rather striking qualifications. They were demonstrated one morning, when the worst theft ever at Palmaille No. 33 was discovered. Probably Simon Bad and helpers had commandeered a furniture van, because they stole no less than twenty Persian rugs, three old Dutch paintings and, not least, a complete set of silverware for thirty-six people. Also purloined were the large collection of filigree and snuffboxes, Granny's pride, and the undamaged nine muses in Meissen porcelain, as well as some of grandfather's suits and other household items. Food also disappeared, including one ham.

Mr. Bad had bored holes in the drawing room beside Granny's bedroom, avoiding noises by working with a piece of soap. Then he sawed a hole into the tabletop to get his own papers, which were locked in the top drawer. Again and again people assured Granny how important it was that she had not heard a thing, because a man like Bad would certainly have shot her on the spot if she had appeared at the door!

This all happened in Altona late in the autumn of 1918, at the end of the First World War, during the uprising against the Kaiser. A fork from the silverware that had disappeared was given as a sample to the police. It also was never seen again. The social and political confusion had added to everything else. The trial planned against my grandparents, who "illegally" owned a ham in the years of severe starvation, did not take place. The case was dismissed. The police suspected that the van with all the stolen goods had crossed the Danish border the same night, because no piece was ever seen again.

All this excitement at a time of great political change was followed by my grandparents' decision that the house at Palmaille No. 33 was too big for two old people to live in and just too difficult to handle. But before they finally moved, a lot still had to happen!

The Elbe, with its ever changing pageant of the seasons, provided a certain connection to nature, as did the magnificent flower arrangements in the house. In spite of this, my grandparents thought, in the end, that their children needed a rural balance to their life in the Palmaille home. After years of searching, in 1890 Grandfather Warburg bought the pretty country house on Baron Voght Street in Klein-Flottbeck, a suburb of Hamburg.

3

Flottbeck

How easy it sounds when somebody says, "I bought myself a house"! A house here or there, large or small, in a garden, with a view of a lake, or a forest, with—with—with. . . . But buying a house is very different from building or renting one. If you build a house, all wishes can be taken into consideration. If you rent a house, you have to decide whether you expect to live there a long time or will change to another one sooner or later. But when you *buy* a house, it really has to be the place you want!

I have no idea how my grandfather found the house in Flottbeck, because at that time I was still in the frog pond, where the babies come from, as you should know. Nobody told me the story when I was young and, if they had, I would not have been interested anyhow. And when I was older, when these problems fascinated me, there was nobody alive anymore who could have told me.

It may have been the flow of the Elbe that attracted my grandparents to follow the stream seaward in their search for a summer mansion. They followed the waterway from the Palmaille on the road to Ottensen, and then high along above Övelgönne, past some large mansions with magnificent gardens and majestic trees. After a long coach trip, the road descends to the "Devils Bridge" and stays at water level. From there a street bends off to the right, along the Jenisch-Park, and with slow horses the coach climbs up Baron Voght Street to the low hill on dry land on which Klein-Flottbeck is situated.

From my grandparents' house one could see the Elbe as a beautiful picture, framed by huge trees. By reading the daily papers carefully, it was easy to know which large oceangoing ships were passing by. And far away over the river there was the broad line of green land, pastures that touched the horizon. The typical North German landscape spread out beyond the stream.

"Flottbeck," as the house was called, was a building in the style called Early Victorian (1830-1841). In German it is called Biedermeier. The house was surrounded by large gardens, and the long building displayed itself best from the garden side, in the shade of large linden and plane trees. Leading to the road were huge groups of old rhododendrons, magnolias with low-hanging branches, and dark trees, as if life had hidden the house from curious passersby. Two large gates opened to the drive, which led semicircularly up to the house and main entrance and brought the carriages back to the road on the other side.

The long building, divided in two equal parts by the centrally placed house door, faced all along the front side with open, glass-covered verandas and thin rails onto the drive-up. They were really asking for the name they were given: the lions' cages. Furnished with Italian cane furniture, covered with bright cushions, the tables with cloths in light shades, it all fit into the coral color of the geraniums in the boxes placed along the length of the house and consequently gave it an air of happiness and luster.

On the left side of the long building there were the living rooms and the pantry, on the right the kitchen, some guest rooms, and a little room for the cook. Like a well-centered little crown the bedrooms of the Warburg family were situated on the first floor. Each room had a terrace from which the various views could be admired. Higher up, under the green copper roof, the servants' rooms could be found, with windows that opened toward the garden. The butler and the coachman had their rooms in the gardener's house, where the stable and the coach hall could be found.

In May the Warburg family, parents and three daughters, moved from the Palmaille to Flottbeck. The old couple went in their victoria, pulled by two black horses, old John on the coachbox. It was always a very enjoyable drive after the end of a successful winter season in town, when it was time to relax in the country. The daughters of the house followed the next day by train from Altona's central station to the Klein-Flottbeck station, where John would get them with the dogcart. It was a great change for the old coachman, because now he did not take grandfather from the Palmaille to the bank twice a day, but only once in the morning to the train, where he picked his master up again at night. It would have been too long a walk for the old gentleman, because it took forty minutes to walk from the house to the train.

A large rented cart with clothes, household goods, preserves, food, the canaries, and the cook arrived a day before the grandparents, because old Frieda had to get everything into working order before her masters arrived. The couple who had looked after Flottbeck in winter moved for the summer into the Palmaille to see that it all was all right for the return of the family in late autumn. This procedure continued into my childhood. Only the riding horses of the young Warburg ladies were not there anymore, and the tennis court was hardly ever used.

At that time Flottbeck was suitable for adults only, and the well-broken-in household management was rather shaken when a new generation began to appear. In 1906 the first grandchild was born to the Warburg grandparents. What a disappointment that I was "only" a girl!

It is said that my father told everybody who was willing to listen that, when I was born, I already had five fingers on each hand and five toes on each foot—a fact that had caused him much astonishment! He had imagined that they might grow later, like teeth. Whether he also told this moving fact to the gentleman at the registration office I do not know.

My birth certificate states only that a daughter was born. Asked for her name, my father did not know any. The family had counted only on a male heir, who, because both grandfathers were called Albert, would carry that name. Only after several days did my parents decide to give me Granny's name, and this was noted down with a later date on the margin of the birth certificate.

My parents enlarged their family by three more children, two sons and a daughter born within the next six years. They had already moved from a small house in the Magdalenenstrasse to a larger one in the Feldbrunnenstrasse. My grandparents decided that these poor town children should enjoy some country life in the summer. Therefore the house in Flottbeck was altered and a new wing added to the right side of the first floor. Every summer the Burchard family moved to Flottbeck with their private staff: a children's nurse and a governess. Although the beautiful symmetry of the building was spoiled, it did not matter in the least, because the tension and anticipation of having the Burchard grandchildren around probably equaled the delight of having the large family in the country.

From the large picture window of the stylish dining room there was a glorious view into the park. This room, with its light furniture, huge flower arrangements, and numerous paintings by Thomas Herbst, especially enchanted all visitors. There was never any talk about the quality of the food, which was always excellent.

One of our childhood pleasures was to ask visitors how many cows they could make out in the paintings in the dining room? The answers varied between fifty-two and fifty-four, and often we could not settle the question whether a rust-red stroke in the background of a picture meant a cow or not. The painter of these landscapes, Thomas Herbst, a friend of the hostess and a frequent guest at Flottbeck, could not answer our questions himself. We thought him rather dull, because he was not open to our childhood interests.

The beautiful dining room was as wonderful to guests as it was a horror to us children. Granny spoiled it to the ground. She placed small mirrors in our water glasses, so that we would be able to watch ourselves while eating. She called our way of eating soup "sliding our mouths open with the spoon." While at table, we were jammed between the armrests of two chairs to which currycombs were attached. These hurt us miserably if we moved farther than permitted. Granny attended to these educational sessions with such tremendous charm that we could not stop loving her dearly, though it was all rather a torment.

That we also adored her so much at table may have its roots in the fact that she let us participate in her table pranks. Only fruits and vegetables from the Flottbeck garden were taken for the meals. In autumn, corn on the cob was often served as an entrée. The butler had waited at table; hot corn on the cob lay on everybody's plate, guests and family members, alike. Granny may have seen this from the corner of her eye. But not everyone knows *how* to get something edible from corn on the cob, which is rarely served in North Germany. Some guests might have thought that chickens would have had it easier, with their beaks; others probably would have been happier if the cob had jumped magically off their plates and back to the plant where it came from. Granny would just continue her intense conversation with her neighbor and seemed not to notice that nobody was eating.

After a while, she would turn to the children at the end of the table and say, "Children, you may begin to eat!" We would then take our corncobs in our left hands, spread them nicely with butter, place the knives on the rim of the plate, grab the cobs with our right hands, and attack them like squirrels. The guests would watch us amazed and fascinated, but only rarely would they have the courage to follow our example, until they saw the lady of the house eating like the grandchildren. "Borgwardt will bring the fingerbowls immediately!" she would add encouragingly.

Both households, the one in the Palmaille and the one in Flottbeck, were run to the minute. Punctuality was asked from everybody. And if somebody was just a little late, Granny would narrow her eyes slightly, as if she were nearsighted, and then look for seconds, which seemed hours, at a grandfather clock, because there was one in every room. That was sufficient. Her motto was *"Exactitude, c'est la politesse des rois."* Punctuality is the politeness of kings!

But the old garden may have been even more beautiful than the house. There were six acres of parkland, joined by two acres of orchards and vegetable gardens, hotbeds and glasshouses. It was a large estate, demanding quite some staff to be kept in the way Granny insisted on: a chief gardener, whose wife looked after the fowl, ducks, geese, turkeys, guinea fowl, and pigeons; two gardeners, who had to attend to every task that came up; and four women, who did easier work, like weeding.

This staff enabled Granny to grow all vegetables in her own garden, and so she brought the first salad in the same perfection to the table as late melons from hotbeds or grapes from the glasshouses. She kept every fig on the south trellis of a glasshouse in mind and watched them carefully, knowing exactly which fruit would ripen first. These were her most personal fruits, and nobody ever found out how such Mediterranean figs would taste straight from the tree, at least not unseen. If anybody tried, Granny always seemed to know who it might have been. He was soon struck by her questioning look and certainly would have given something *if* he could have hung up the forbidden fruit again.

Every morning, rather early, Granny went through the vegetable garden with the cook to plan the provisions for the household on the spot. The chief gardener, Brüllau, then opened his knife and cut the lettuce, cauliflower, and other vegetables to which Granny pointed. The vegetables then lay on the rim of the beds, and later one of the gardenwomen brought them into the kitchen.

It was one of Granny's great pleasures to walk along the asparagus beds to find out how many tips were thriving into the light. Where there were cracks in the soil, she drew small circles around the center of the cracks, so that Brüllau could find the asparagus more easily. Years earlier Brüllau had lost his wedding ring while working somewhere in the garden. After several years, an asparagus top pushed the ring back into the light, so he too had a special liking for that part of his domain.

Not far from this part of the vegetable garden, in the shade of some gooseberry bushes, were some lilies of the valley. Whenever Granny was there at blossom time, she took a few stems and pressed them into one of their leaves, as into a sheltering small umbrella. When she enjoyed the scent of these tiny flowers, there was a very special smile on her face. Was it a memory which overcame her? Who knows? The graciousness with which she then fastened the little bunch of flowers to her blouse came from a time that is long past.

There were trellises of roses, mainly crimson ramblers, leading from the house into the flower garden, where annuals and perennials created a mosaic of multitudinous colors. In this part of the garden, Granny enjoyed herself most. She would be dressed in a simple cotton frock. A large straw hat would be on her head. She tied it at her chin with a huge bow on the left side, to shelter her complexion. She would carry a large flat basket on her arm, and a pair of shears in her hand, as she walked along the flower beds. These clothes mirrored Granny's love for the Impressionist painters. And, for me, my Granny was then the personification of a Renoir portrait.

Slowly and dreamily she walked along, enjoying, choosing, cutting flowers—flowers for the numerous vases in the house, for bunches to be given to departing guests, or to be sent to hospitals during the war. Returning to the house, she went with her basket into the pantry, choosing carefully which flowers to use for a certain purpose, and arranging them with artistic taste.

During the last summer before the First World War, my grandparents spent some time in Monte Carlo, and Granny insisted on visiting the Casino to try her luck. Grandfather, serious and well mannered as was his way, did not think it proper and did not permit it. But after a few days he changed his mind and wanted to give her the pleasure of a try with one twenty-Mark gold piece. Granny won at roulette, won and won again, very much to grandfather's pain. Now, what to do with that much money, how to spend it? Granny had an idea. She would get something for the grandchildren!

A Riviera jenny-donkey was acquired and sent by train to

Flottbeck, across Europe. We called her Lotte, and she joined the sheep, goats, and the cow in the fenced-in meadow. She also shared the shed with them, looking for shelter when it rained, and she got used to the North German hay. But she soon showed the moods of her Italian character, because she had no desire to be saddled or harnessed. She placed herself behind the old he-goat, Hans, put her head on his back, and gave an unfriendly kick to the back. But the butler, Borgwardt, managed her easily because Lotte forgot all aversions when she took a sugarloaf from his flat hand. This was the moment when he grabbed her halter.

We all learned to ride on Lotte's back and had her pull a pretty little carriage around the garden. It was a children's circus! Borgwardt looked on proudly.

For many years Lotte led the life of a luxury jenny. The world war changed her way of life. The elegant small carriage was not used anymore; a small cart followed, and Lotte had to work. The garden "went to war"; the lawns were dug over and potatoes planted. The grass in the usually well-cut English lawn in front of the house could now grow at leisure, producing enough "hay" for Lotte's winter supply. Lotte had to bring potatoes to the cellars and hay to the sheds, had to pull the cart with cow manure to the potato patches, and had to do other agricultural work.

One day Borgwardt, who had always kept a sheltering hand over Lotte, left for military service. With his departure something special went out of our childhood life. Lotte died soon after. A heavily loaded cart of potatoes was too much for her to pull uphill. Lotte's death was the first real deep grief in our childhood. Father tried to solace us. He spoke of Lotte's immortality, saying she would live as a part of the Christmas candles. We thought this still worse than the simple burial of our donkey.

Buying the jenny did not exhaust the Monte Carlo money. The local Flottbeck carpenter got an order to build a large doll's house. One side of it was intended for the croquet game and gymnastic equipment. The other side held a marvelous doll's kitchen and our garden furniture. All this was for our pleasure, and for the delight of our cousins and many other children. A real small iron kitchen stove stood in the corner. It had come from Granny's childhood in Holland. Stoked with wood, the stove had a chimney high over the doll's house roof. We were really able to cook on the open hearth holes, and on the side there was a brass water tank, which we kept well polished. Saucepans of various sizes and shapes hung on the wall; so did small frying pans. Granny's sisters had given us a very pretty set of china, manufactured in Vienna. On the rim of the small cups and saucers, plates and bowls, there were dwarfs with pointed hats, dancing or playing with frogs, squirrels, or mice, and other charming and funny scenes that delighted our young hearts.

During peacetime we were permitted to get the cooking ingredients from the cook, and she was always very generous. During the war our chances dwindled. The adults called it "playing with foodstuffs," and that was a crime; they kept their supplies. But we were permitted to cook with the eggs of our small hen, and a bit of flour and fat helped us bake small pikelets, approximately three inches in diameter. The accompanying fruit we were allowed to get in the garden, and we stewed it in our largest saucepan on the little stove.

In a very hidden corner of the large garden grandfather built a studio for his gifted and very much admired wife. It was a pretty wooden construction with satisfactory side and top windows. In this secluded place Granny could paint to her heart's content. Nobody was permitted to disturb her there, and nobody could enter without permission. The greatest pleasure we could give Granny was to make her a present of "sittings"—times when we would allow her to paint us. And because I was often alone with her in her studio, I noticed where she hung the key: on a nail under the gutter.

One day, when I knew Granny was in Altona, the devil pushed me to inspect the studio on my own. With wildly beating heart I took the key down and unlocked the door, which creaked nastily when I opened it very slowly. It was very quiet in the large place. But I could hear the bees buzz. Their round hives stood along the south wall of the studio, in the sun. All oils were turned with their painted side to the wall. A portrait of me stood on the easel.

The pictures did not interest me very much, but the life-size clay figure of our laundress, the head of which I had seen already, caught my attention at once. The body was covered by a piece of cloth. The face, the parted hair, and the small bun on the back of her head showed much resemblance. Because I was alone in the studio now, I had the courage to take the cloth off Mrs. Jones. How I wished I had not risked it! Mrs. Jones was absolutely naked, holding her arms with the big laundress's hands folded under enormous breasts, which she seemed to squeeze flat. What a hideous sight, I thought. Above all, I was ashamed of Mrs. Jones for showing herself in such a state to grandmother, and because Granny, *my* Granny, had shaped something so hideous from clay!

As quickly as possible, I dressed Mrs. Jones again, silently closed the door of the studio, hung the key on the nail, and was glad that our big black tomcat crossed my way. With him on my arm I climbed into one of our favorite trees and petted my lost balance back into me from his shiny fur.

A robin, which might not have noticed the cat, hopped around in the branches, making soft noises. While I stroked the cat, observing the bird at the same time, a tale Granny had once told me crossed my mind. She told it when I was rather distressed about a dead bird I had shown her. I wondered whether it had fallen from the nest or whether another little bird might have pushed it out.

"Well, my child, it will be good to learn in early days that there always will be a stronger power in the world. It all works out the same: A man shoots a cat because it hunts his favorite little birds; he praises the Lord, who gave him the power to use the gun. The cat catches, kills, and eats the bird and thanks the Lord for the good meal. The bird scratches the soil and finds a little worm that it eats, then thanks the Lord for his good vision, which provided the delicacy. And now comes the question: Did the worm also sing when he had the pleasure of being eaten by the bird, and did he thank the Lord for the honor of disappearing in the birdie's crop? If you have the time, you may give this problem a thought, Gertrud."

When she told me this story, I silently strolled away. Now, with the cat in my arms, perched high in the tree, thinking about it, I still could not get any solution. When the gong called for dinner, I had forgotten both Mrs. Jones and the little worm.

In Flottbeck the gong rang twice before every meal. The first sound meant that the meal would be served ten minutes later; the children had to wash their hands. I always ran into the house so fast that I could do this in the downstairs WC, beside the back entrance. I loved this place, because of the old blue Dutch tiles on the walls. I had counted twenty-three different subjects: many varieties of farmhouses, windmills, small bridges, sailboats, biblical stories, and various single animals. I had never been able to find out in which sequence, or better in which untidy way, the walls had been tiled. This inequality fascinated me and often kept me impermissibly long in that place.

In this way I was once late at table. Everybody had already started on the soup. Since there were no guests, Granny asked where I had been to come so late.

"Where even an emperor goes alone" was my answer, because we were not allowed to speak of this certain place.

"What did you do there as long as that?"

"Counting swans," I answered in a very low voice.

"Come here, Gertrud, give me a kiss! I see clearly that you are *my* granddaughter and a quarter Dutch! Your interest in tiles shows it very well. Next time, please begin to count your swans earlier!"

The First World War changed Flottbeck right away, and destroyed it almost totally by the end of 1917. The garden furniture and all the wooden fences were cut to pieces during the night, for firewood. Fruit was picked before it was ripe, the vines and the fig tree were killed by frost during the wartime winters, and the tender sun of spring could not call them back to life after they had been in unheated glasshouses for years.

But Granny did not give in, because she had the chance to help feed her eight grandchildren. (Ada Sophie Warburg married a few years later than her elder sister, Ellen, and also had four children.) Granny was allowed to keep one cow, which lived a normal cow life in Flottbeck. But in the autumn of 1918 this animal was transported to the Palmaille. There, some wide boards had been placed over the stairs to the basement. The cook pulled the poor beast by its halter, the coachman pushed from the back, and so the cow got into a small cellar beside the laundry. One of Granny's maids traveled daily by train from Altona to Hamburg and back, carrying a milk container, which in turn Aunt Ada's or our maid took over, exchanging it for an empty one.

Shortly before the end of the war, the cow had a calf in the cellar of the Palmaille. The poor creature was slaughtered very quietly without police authorization, so it had a very inglorious but for all of us nourishing end.

Flottbeck as well as the Palmaille were sold before Christmas of 1918. New regulations did not permit one family to live in two houses. Grandfather was not well enough to live in Flottbeck only. It was too difficult and slow to get medical help out there. And the house at Palmaille No. 33 was unmanageable for two old people. Also the problems with domestic help were such at that time that continued living in that big house made no sense. My grandparents therefore moved into an apartment in the Hotel Esplanade in Hamburg, where my grandfather Albert Warburg died on February 19, 1919, at seventy-six.

I was thirteen when Granny took my hand and very silently led me into grandfather's bedroom. I saw him lying very quiet and pale on his bed. His eyes were closed and he held a small bunch of violets in his hands, which were joined on his chest.

"Have a last look at him, Gertrud," Granny said. "He is so beautiful when he is asleep."

She led me from the room, sat down at the high window of their hotel drawing room, and pulled me on her knees. Together we watched how the sky became red over Hamburg's Botanical Gardens. To me only a daily sun sank. But Granny's life darkened after the loss of her companion.

That late afternoon she made a remark she was going to repeat to me in darkest times: "Stick to nature, Gertrud. Nature will never grieve you!"

4

Interlude

Granny decided to move near her two married daughters. She was looking forward to seeing her eight grandchildren grow up and to being close to them. She would also try to overcome the great loss of her husband. She intended to be a grandmother first of all.

Compared to her former house, the one she chose, Hochallee No. 5, Hamburg-Rothenbaum, was certainly small and humble. But it was large enough to permit some alterations in the course of time.

My grandparents' youngest daughter, Betty, lost the man of her heart during the war and stayed unmarried. Very much against the inclination of Grandfather Warburg, who—as was the attitude of his time—thoroughly disliked educated women, Aunt Betty studied medicine and got through her examinations with honors. The old gentleman thought it not very decent for a young lady of high social standing to survey dead bodies as a profession.

After the death of the old gentleman and the move of Granny and Aunt Betty to the Hochallee, the question was solved as to whether it would be more economical to start a new medical practice and earn some money, or to save on domestic help. For the time being, the practice was not started. So the two ladies' first years in the new house were extremely quiet and secluded, mainly because of their financial status.

Only very little of the furniture of two large houses could be placed in the new home. Because all the large old Dutch paintings could not be hung in the small rooms, only four remained. For the time being, Granny gave the others into the custody of the Rijksmuseum in Amsterdam, her home town, but later, as an expression of her strong tie with Holland, she made the museum a gift of all paintings being held there.

It was as if Granny wanted to announce this new period of her life in a special way: she decorated the Hochallee house with contemporary paintings. The remaining four Dutch portraits stayed close to her in her bedroom. They were pictures from her parental home, familiar since her youth, and they may have been something like a protective cloak to her.

Soon after her husband's death, Granny became a Dutch citizen again. The estate was left to her. After her death, her three daughters would have it, and it would be divided only among the eight grandchildren. A well-known lawyer and international financier was the executor, and friends would advise the widow. Grandfather's will was made in the Hamburg way; it tried to settle all problems for time and eternity.

But the change of nationality made Granny a foreigner, living in Germany. All money transactions were subject to the regulations of the Foreign Exchange Department. The administration of the will put the amount necessary to buy the house at Hochallee No. 5 at Granny's disposal. Buying this place was the first personal business transaction of the widow Warburg, at the age of sixty-three.

"Everything has its time," I heard Granny say very often. She never looked back when material problems had to be tackled. In her little household, with its exquisite damask linen, the silverware and the old Meissen porcelain, the Palmaille continued to exist, in a small way. Friends were therefore inclined to believe that she was still well-to-do, and it gave her great pleasure to let them believe this.

Meals in her house were always exquisite. To prepare them,

a former cook came for the night, and a maid who had served in the family for many years came to attend at table. But with the currency devaluation things got more and more difficult, and the means for hospitality became smaller and smaller. It happened that the ladies Warburg had to eat potatoes and salted herrings for the rest of the week, just after having served a luscious dinner to some friends.

The inflation had brought the estate of Albert Warburg down to a tenth of what it had been at his death. Clever administration had managed things so that Granny could make a moderate living. But when times worsened further, the income of her sons-in-law became insufficient to provide for their families. Granny then divided her income into four equal parts and gave each of her daughters one-fourth as pin money. The last quarter she kept for herself. Because Aunt Betty lived with her, they managed together to make ends meet.

All this happened very quietly, so that no outsider had any idea of the things that happened. Granny assumed a new role on the stage of life, and she liked herself in this part.

I became aware of this one evening while I was waiting for her to finish a letter so that I could mail it on my way home. Granny opened a drawer to get some stamps. In front there were quite a number of old, rather worn purses. I asked what they meant.

"You see, Gertrud, I live like an officer's widow!" Granny explained. "She divides her pension nicely. After the bank sends me my monthly money, the dividing begins. The household money is in this purse. In this one is a certain amount for heating, water and light, so that there is enough when the bills come in. And in this little one I accumulate small amounts for clothing. Of course, we first have to wear all we have, but shoes have to be soled, clothes to be dry-cleaned, and so forth. And this purse, which once was your grandfather's, is for something very special. It is called 'PLEASURE' and I try to branch off as much as I can into this one, as traveling also belongs in the pleasure purse! And tonight, Gertrud, it is my pleasure to make you a present of five Marks!"

After dinner I often went to see Granny. The houses at

Hochallee and Feldbrunnenstrasse were only ten minutes apart, and whenever anyone dropped in at Granny's she was either engaged in writing letters, playing solitaire, or knotting fine filet nets. She always made these nets, similar to those that the fishermen knotted on the shores of her parental Dutch land. Her poor eyesight did not permit finer needlework. These nets would later be narrowly gathered and sewn around small pieces of cloth, to decorate bread baskets, and would be given away to members of the family or her numerous acquaintances.

This modest creation of lace-like things led to a beautiful collection. Granny's mother had owned and collected laces. She divided them among her daughters, who all added pieces to their part. Granny had quite a collection. It was not dated or labeled, but was tidily placed in boxes covered with silk. They stood in a certain wardrobe. Granny knew a lot about laces and I had to learn much from her. So already in my early years I handled the beautiful pieces, which are now mine. I had to date them with the help of a magnifying glass, which is done by recognizing the way the ground nets are worked.

I also heard about the historical background of the pieces: how lacemakers emigrated from Italy, where lacemaking began, to France, where, during the reign of Louis XIV, the lacemakers were settled in various parts of the country. The finance minister Colbert brought this craft over the Alps, because the luxury at the French court had become so costly that the royal finances could no longer afford laces imported from Italy. It was much cheaper to establish lacemaking centers in the north. During the religious persecution, the lacemakers came to the British Isles where there had been no national craft in that line before. Granny told me such stories when I visited her in the evenings. While she talked, her needle went back and forth indefatigably.

I also remember a story that reached into our century: In 1914, just before the First World War, Granny sent some old laces, which she tried to preserve, to Brussels, to have them mended and cleaned by a well-known manufacturing firm. She had forgotten all about this, when, soon after the end of the war, her laces were sent in a registered parcel with a bill. In an accompanying letter the hope was expressed that the parcel would find the owner in the best of health.

Wherever we traveled in our youth, Granny visited markets and looked around secondhand shops searching for laces and old embroidery, which she bought cheaply. She was always extremely proud of her "finds." Back home in Hamburg, she would examine the pieces with the magnifying glass, and then they would be repaired. This repairing was called: Gertrud. It certainly was not one of my happiest moments as a fifteen-year-old girl, to darn fine laces with No. 200 thread and an unbelievably fine needle. At this time Granny's eyesight had already rapidly dwindled, while my facility increased fast. However, since I was such a great help to Granny, these hours together became a pleasure for both of us.

Every night Granny wrote a letter to her younger sister in Berlin. And every night the letter had to be mailed. Often I had to wait until the letter was finished. The sisters were as quarrelsome as they were close, and their meetings were not always harmonious. Granny once noted this state of affairs with an unforgettable remark: "Better a good letter than a bad meeting!"

Such remarks stuck in the memory of a young person, though the deep meaning and the wisdom within were understood only by her grown-up granddaughter. The same is true of a motto that Granny wrote in a leather-bound diary she gave me in 1922. She meant the diary to accompany me all my life, and she was certain that all blank pages would be filled with quotations from books I was going to read. She herself wrote on the first page:

> *Learn to accept with ever more gratitude*
> *and to give with ever more gaiety.*
>
> LAVATER

She hoped that the thoughts that had crystallized in other people's expressions would reflect my own way of thinking. And so that nobody else would be able to get at these most treasured ideas, there was a lock on the side of the black book. The key has been lost for many many years, but sometimes I still leaf through the pages, shaking my head as I read the dates on which the quotations were copied.

In the same year—and this is also marked in the book—Granny became very ill. One day she had given mother a call, asking her to send me over at once after school, because she needed me. Even before I could inquire about her health, she gave me her bunch of keys from her night table and in a very low voice asked me to hand her a box from a certain wardrobe in the room. I placed a large carton on her bed. She opened it carefully and took out the death mask and the plaster casts of the hand of her son, who had died at age seven. She held them up and looked at them, perhaps with death before her eyes. She held a silent dialogue with her child, who had left her thirty-one years before that day.

I stood behind her bed and cried. Cried because my Granny was so tremendously sad, and in gratitude for the confidence that she gave me again and again.

———

In 1924 the purse marked "Pleasure" must have been well filled, because Granny invited my brother Albert, two years my junior, and me to accompany her to Italy. We would participate in an "art excursion," as she called it. At Christmas we found a small watercolor painting, a sketch Granny had painted for the occasion. It showed cypresses and stone pines throwing hard shadows on a sun-drenched landscape. This roused our expectations no end!

At that time there were still three different classes in the railways. To save money, Granny and I traveled second class, and Albert third class. He preferred this anyhow, because his traveling companions were undoubtedly much more amusing than ours.

Rome! During six weeks of holidays, nothing but Rome. Six weeks of hard work under Granny's watchful eye. Every morning sightseeing with a guide, who had to give a written statement that we had been with him, so that we could not break away and do something else. Then we had lunch, a siesta, and in the afternoon Granny herself took us through some museums. We were so overfed with art of every description that we saved the Forum Romanum for the last day, since we were certain that, if there was still time enough, we would be forced to go there several times. So it was only too understandable that Albert took a stone from one of the goldsmiths' workshops in the Forum and smashed it on Granny's table. This meant: Enough with all learning and sightseeing in Rome! But then came a surprise.

Without showing her excitement, Granny turned to me and said, "Gertrud, you are going to call for a taxi at once. Without lunch you both drive to the Forum, and Albert replaces the stone in exactly the same spot where he *stole* it! What are you thinking, you desecrators, which you are! And as punishment Albert is going to recite in English language six times Brutus' funeral oration for Caesar—and you, Gertrud—you will watch it closely that he does not do it only *five* times! Here is the money. Let the taxi wait at the Forum, and when all is done, return here at once!"

This all happened the last day we were in Rome, on the afternoon on which Granny had promised to have a good cup of coffee with us in an elegant place on the Pincio.

During the night in the Holy City, Rome did not take any revenge on Granny, but did not give her a good rest either. Because we shared the same room, I wished I could help her in her restlessness, but I did not know how. Whatever may have tormented Granny, neither one of us got any sleep, because Rome was shaken by a slight earthquake, which we could both feel while we were in bed.

Granny at once switched on her bedside lamp, leaned out of her bed, and said with a trembling voice "You down there under my bed, come out! Come out immediately, you thief. I have seen you for a long time!"

It was just this genuine mixture of enthusiasm for the arts and a humane way of looking at things that made many travels with Granny so memorable.

While we traveled with Granny, Aunt Betty stayed home. She always found some excuse: the canaries had to be looked after, the garden needed watering, and so on. Only much later did I understand that she wanted to save the costs that her participation would have involved. To enable her mother to go on these trips with her grandchildren, enjoying herself no end, Aunt Betty was hard on herself.

In November of 1926 Granny reached the age of seventy. The family had planned gifts, displays by the grandchildren, and a dinner. She countered the onslaught of such suggestions with just one wish, expressed to adults and children alike. From each member of the family she demanded an essay on the question "What does real culture entail?"

How two generations mastered this tricky question, and around whose forehead Granny placed an imaginary laurel wreath, I can no longer remember.

5

Three Generations of Burchards

The family ties connecting us with the Warburg grandparents were so close that all our childhood affections and all the wonderfully deep feelings for an old generation fully belonged only to them. The Burchard grandparents moved only in the 1920s from Berlin to Hamburg, to pass their old age close to their married sons. As I grew up with stories and tales from the Warburg house, I remember only very few that I was told from the Burchard family.

Grandfather Burchard, born on February 10, 1845, in Breslau, followed the example of his father, who was a medical practitioner and obstetrician. During his studies he traveled on foot to Würzburg to attend medical lectures there. At the border of his native Silesia he had to change his Silesian thalers into the currency of his university province. At that time this was done in the office of a notary public. This old gentleman always asked the young student, "Dear young friend, what do you intend to do with all that money?" I expect that the old notary may then have told his young client to be very careful with all the golden coins he now had, because it would have cost my great-grandfather much bloodletting and the use of many leeches to earn that amount.

When he came to the end of the university term and nearly

to the end of the talers, and when hunger started to hurt, there was still a way to get some cheap food in Würzburg. A well-known student pub offered all that was needed. One had to descend into a dark cellar. A dim oil lamp hung from the ceiling. Nearly the whole place was taken up by a huge long table with numerous stools all around it. Hollows were carved into the tabletop, one in front of every stool. Beside the hollow, a spoon was fastened with a chain. At a certain time of the day one could go into the cellar, take a place on a stool, and wait for things to happen.

If a sufficient number of customers were seated, the host of the pub arrived, followed by a kitchen boy, who carried a huge steaming pewter pot. The host then asked each customer whether he wanted soup for five cents or for ten cents. After hearing the decision, he sucked the soup noisily from the pewter pot with a huge syringe. He then put pressure on his implement and filled the hollow with soup. One of the great pranks of the students was to ask for ten-cent soup and then pay only five cents. The infuriated host then placed the syringe back in the hollow and sucked back half the soup, up to a painted mark.

Grandfather Burchard was said always to have been such an efficient and hard-working student that he could follow his inclination to become an eye specialist. To improve his manual skill for work in eye operations, he copied exceptionally detailed oil paintings by Johannes Heinrich Wilhelm Tischbein and his contemporaries, using his left hand.

In 1870 Albert August Burchard was old enough to fight for his country in the Franco-Prussian war of 1870 to 1871. His bride-to-be was Anna Maria Auguste Hermine Windmüller. The daughter of a Breslau banker, she was born on July 18, 1850. Now, she feared for Albert's life. The young people were engaged. They intended to wait for the end of the war and then get married, because the young hero had finished his medical examinations before entering military service. One day this most wonderful of all men under the sun returned from the battlefield and told of the red-trousered Zouaves he had routed with his sword! Young Anna's heart beat faster and faster, until on October 20, 1872, she was given away to her beloved eye doctor.

Already in his youth the future Sanitätsrat Dr. Med. had a special custom. Three times a day he checked the outside temperature and noted it in a log. The barometer reading was also noted. When we were young, we could not give the old gentleman a greater pleasure than asking him what the weather had been on a certain day in, say, 1881. He would give the answer at once.

Just as pedantically as he made his meteorological observations, he made a note of the outcome of the three games of solitaire he played every evening after dinner. If they did not all come out, he did not sleep well. Everything was well organized with him, his sleep as well.

The grandparents from Breslau had three children, one daughter and two sons. Their second child, Edgar Eduard Walter Burchard, was born on July 6, 1879. He became my father.

In my youth Grandfather Burchard was already a rather old gentleman and a widower as well. He lived with us in our house on the Feldbrunnenstrasse. He always had a special way of preparing for a trip. On the day before his departure, he left the house at exactly the same time as he would the following day to catch his train. He bought a platform ticket and waited with flying havelock collar for the train. From his left shoulder on a long leather strap hung a large purse; in his right hand he held a traveling bag with a cross-stitch embroidered "Happy Journey" decoration. When at long last the train came in, he cautiously walked along the carriages and chose a first-class compartment that was not over the springs. After having found the place of his choice, he took a piece of white chalk from his huge purse on the leather strap and marked the position of his compartment on the floor of the platform. This enabled him to find his way easily the next day. He then walked home with the pride of a commander in chief who has worked out his battle plan to the last detail.

To his last day old Grandfather Burchard kept his underwear tidily separated in his wardrobe by drawing chalk lines to give socks, shirts, and singlets their proper place. He also had the strange habit of blowing his nose for the first time into a clean handkerchief, always using the corner opposite the monogram first. He died in 1933 at eighty-eight.

———

My parents, Dr. iur. Edgar Eduard Burchard and Helene Julie (Ellen) Warburg, were married on May 23, 1905, in the St. Katharinen Church in Hamburg. They spent the first period of their marriage on the island of Helgoland, where the young solicitor was transferred to check the register of land property. It was the custom there that mortgages could be taken on each floor of a building, and this nuisance had to be finished with. If a theft or other crime happened on the island, father was the legal authority, and mother, as the sole and only member of the public, followed the actions of her young and beloved husband closely and full of pride.

Because my father was sent to Helgoland before finishing his legal studies, he returned to Kiel after completing his work in Helgoland. And so I appeared at the beginning of March 1906 in Kiel, very much to the sorrow of my parents and later myself, who so very much would have preferred to have been born a proper Hamburgian! Though I was taken from Kiel to Hamburg when only a few months old, in a comfortable laundry basket, it has never been easy for me to write "born in Kiel." I would have preferred "born in Hamburg."

In a small house on the Magdalenenstrasse the following three Burchard offspring were born. The family life of such a typically Hamburgian family ran in an absolutely prescribed way, with its servants and educational personnel. Father left the house early to walk to his office, and the governess took us for an early walk, accompanying the head of the family along the Alster River. On the way home, we fed some swans from the Rabenstrassenbrücke. If father left the house very early, to row before going to town, we were very sad, because it was too early for us to accompany him. Father's private skiff lay in the Hamburger Ruderclub, where the Hamburg elite gathered for this sport.

Sometimes we also accompanied the old nurse Trinchen to the lake side, where she sat in the sun and crocheted wide lace borders for the sun curtains, the pram with the youngest Burchard by her side. Asked by promenading passersby to whom the pretty baby and the elegant perambulator belonged, she used to answer full of pride, "It is a Warburg grandchild!" Her employers the Burchards, she felt, were not important enough!

We adored our father, because he was a *real* father. When we were small, he played with us on the floor and could invent wonderful stories. He told us of the zebras, who would rub off their black stripes on the rubber trees, and then they would hide as small white horses when the animal catchers of the well-known Hagenbeck Zoo wanted to catch zebras. He tried to explain why the behinds of the baboons were so ugly: This was useful, because their names were written in phosphorescent paint, so that they would find each other at night in the dark jungle.

Sometimes, when the noise in the nursery was too much and when father played with us and got to the stage of crumpled suit and open tie, mother appeared in the door, beautifully dressed, a lady from top to toe. She had heard fragments from father's wonderful stories and would repeat a remark we had often heard: "Edgar, please do not muddle up the thoughts of the children!"

Kindness and vehemence were mixed in father. So it is understandable that mother feared he could harm his children if he handed out some physical punishment, since he had exceptional strength. As soon as father lifted a hand, mother threw herself between him and the evildoer and we always heard the same outcry: "Edgar, you will hit the children so that they may be crippled for life!"

When mother stood with her arms wide open between the two parties, father regained his balance, put his arms around her neck and began to cry bitterly, realizing his irascibility. That all this did not add a positive influence to our education is more than understandable, I think.

At the beginning of World War I, the old walnut tree in our back garden was called up for military service, as was father. The latter stayed in the rear, because of his weak eyes. The walnut tree got into the front lines; its wood was used for rifle butts.

After the war, we moved into the house at Feldbrunnenstrasse No. 21, which seemed large enough for teenagers.

One may get the impression that the four Burchard children, heirs to half the considerable estate of the banker Albert Warburg, grew up fed with a silver spoon. That certainly was not so. Probably the main difference from today was the fact that material goods had little importance. On weekdays we wore blue-white striped sailor suits for the boys and frocks for the girls, and the same in white on Sundays, which was fashionable and practical at the same time. Our food was adjusted to three mottoes:

1. To eat and to drink holds body and soul together.
2. One eats to stay alive, but one does not live to eat.
3. Gluttons are not born, but reared.

First our education was in the hands of nurses, later of governesses, also English and French ones, who gave us the basic knowledge of languages.

We were not exceptionally good scholars, just average pupils. Father had a description of our reports: "Passing—O.K.!" Because of an inherited eagerness and industriousness, I, the eldest of four, passed without repeating a grade. Not so my brothers, of whom father charmingly commented, "My son—— was so interested in his class that he decided to take it again!"

At the end of the war, when there was no coal to heat the schools, it was great fun to have all four classes in our large dining room, since we still had some fuel. The blackboard stood on the grand piano, and during the breaks the teacher had to go out of the room and spend the recreation time in the hall.

So our life at Feldbrunnenstrasse No. 21 began rather pleasantly and without worries, though also without any luxury at all. The inflation and the rapid devaluation suddenly shook the domestic balance. For some reason father gave up law. but he could not find other work. This depressed him deeply, and in the end he became very sick indeed.

The family's financial difficulties meant that Granny and Aunt Betty skimped still more. The money that Granny had divided among her daughters and herself was almost gone. She began to sell some of her works of art. It was just ballast, she said easily; food was more important. Up to then, father had always been able to cheer Granny up. Now it was the old lady who managed to pull her son-in-law out of a deep depression.

When we were young, we would have loved to see our kind and quiet mother sitting at our bedside at night, reading us a story. But governesses took her place. Father, everywhere adored as a charming entertainer, loved to go out and wanted his beautiful and elegant wife to share his position in Hamburg high society. Our parents often came into our bedrooms before going out, and we admired them in dinner jacket and beautiful evening dress. We thought it wonderful to take in the scent of mother's perfume when she kissed us good night. But this pretty picture also changed with the inflation; it was just wiped out, and the friendly, harmonious marriage of my parents became a union of shared fate.

All the governesses and maids got sacked, and only the old cook stayed with us. Mother put on a huge apron herself and began to reorganize the house. She had decided to rent rooms to earn money for the household. Her effort, determination, and ability made it possible to rent rooms to Englishmen "during the twenties," which meant payment in foreign currency with stable values. Then mother began to wash and iron for her tenants and kept their clothes in order—work that further increased her income for the household. So my parents managed, between them, to get past the most difficult financial time that Germany had after the war.

It is understandable that under these conditions mother had no time to survey her children's schoolwork. She was probably persuaded that we would do our best in school to support the parental efforts for survival in our own way. She probably also thought us extremely gifted and capable of managing school outside and work at home. So the "blue letters" that arrived suddenly were an additional hardship to mother, because they meant that my brothers would not be transferred to the next class. She had to see the schoolmaster and her sons' teachers—a task that was very hard on her. Father was not impressed and told his sons that he too had not been a good pupil and that he too had once had to repeat a grade. This knowledge undermined the small remnant of authority that father still had, and he never got it back, which he did not mind a bit.

But in the end Albert and Oswald managed their Abitur (graduation), and both began business training. Granny as well as the old Sanitätsrat Dr. Burchard deplored that none of the Burchard boys ever would "wear the hat," which meant a doctor's degree.

Marie, the youngest, successfully finished Miss Henckel's secondary school and continued her studies in the Industrial School of Arts, where she met a man who greatly influenced her life.

It is often said that the eldest child of larger families gets a stricter education than the younger ones. I cannot say this about myself. To Granny and to my father, to whom I was especially close, it was rather astonishing that there was a young member of the family who turned out to be absolutely different. They watched me with patience and never even tried to interfere.

It is always easiest for parents if their children develop their own interests. To Granny's amazement, I began to go in a probably inherited direction, which Grandfather Burchard had always fostered—the study of nature. Although Granny had inculcated the love of art into me since childhood, a delight in nature long remained my most important inclination. To me, nature was not only Granny's way of seeing it as beauty; to me it also meant knowledge!

Therefore I think that Granny looked at my further activities with a certain mixture of astonishment and pity: From the garden shed I got a flat basket, in which there certainly had once been a beautiful flower arrangement, and filled it carefully with moss. Then I roamed the garden and collected all species of mushrooms I could find, placed them carefully in the moss, labeled them neatly, and took them to school. As I paraded with the basket on the train platform, some old gentlemen nodded toward the young girl in a friendly way. I knew them all, because they were always the same. Some had rosebuds in their buttonholes, and others carnations.

Then the period of my insect collection began in Flottbeck. From my weekly pocket money I bought insect pins, peat slabs, and chemicals to kill the poor creatures. Probably it was the height of Granny's disgust when one of the gardeners made me a present of a cockroach, carefully kept in a matchbox. But Granny already saw an invasion of these "filthy creatures" into her perfectly kept house, I imagine! She simmered down only when I showed her the dead insect, a pin neatly through its thorax. Father, on the other hand, was just as upset when I showed him a hornet, which might have killed me, as he stressed. Only when I came home drenched, after a fall in a pond during an attempt to catch a certain waterbeetle, did mother box my ears for the first time. But all these experiences did not impede my interests.

So, understandably, I began to study natural science after finishing school. But this was possible only if I were able to earn the necessary money myself. The parental purse could not stand the additional drain of a child in the university. And, since there were always children who needed coaching and whose parents were willing to pay for this, I managed to earn what I needed.

In 1925 father again got a position that enabled him to earn enough to relieve mother from renting rooms. My parents were granted a mortgage from the Albert Warburg estate and altered the second floor at Feldbrunnenstrasse No. 21 in such a way that it could be rented as a unit to a young couple.

About the same time, Aunt Betty decided to begin a medical practice to support Granny. The administration of grandfather's estate granted Granny a mortgage for alterations in her house at Hochallee No. 5. The ground floor was altered and a consultation and waiting room for patients was built. And one day passersby would read, on a white enamel plate on the garden door, that Dr. med. Betty Warburg would be available as medical practitioner at fixed hours of the day.

Now a tragedy began. An old, good, and well-known name

became her undoing. Well-to-do people laughed and thought it rather ridiculous that someone with the Warburg name was going to work for money. Simple people supposed that the Warburg name might bring them into contact with a lady who would not understand them, and consequently they were reluctant to ring the bell and walk in.

How well I remember Aunt Betty waiting for patients during her consultation time, wearing a white coat. Often I was with her when she was desperate because nobody came. She needed somebody to talk to; even a young girl like me became her close friend. In the end she started to work on me. She examined me again and again. But when she started to paint red arteries and blue veins all over my chest, I thought this was going too far and objected. So her pain became mine and I witnessed how Betty Warburg found out that it was pretty hard to earn some money.

Then the change came. Members of the family, former employees, tradesmen and their families came and consulted the lady doctor. In the beginning this may have been due to curiosity, but soon they valued and honored her medical knowledge. The number of her patients increased, and her card index, at first so small, grew fast. And every success in her work resulted in a charming smile from the usually so serious, lonely woman. Her practice brought her fulfillment and happiness, which were lacking in her personal life, because the man she had loved was killed in action during the First World War.

After Dr. Med. Betty Warburg was admitted to work for the Medical Benefit Scheme, she was also able to answer calls outside of the house and even tended sick people at night. She helped a pregnant woman or a worker suffering pains after a factory accident. All this was a source of deep satisfaction to her. She was also happy to meet plain people she had never known in her former life. Later, much later, reciprocity occurred: plain people helped her in her own time of need.

6

Strange Words and
Strange Conceptions

In our home there was never any talk about religion. Father, who grew up under the watchful eye of his austere Protestant father, never made any use of his religious tradition. If visitors talked about these subjects at table, nobody took any notice of their ideas, and if religious tracts were left at the door, father crumpled them up and with an embarrassed smile, threw them in the wastebasket.

All these were tiny happenings, which seemed to be totally unimportant, but they occasionally gave mother distant, dreamy thoughts. Then father would carefully put his hand on her shoulder and cautiously say, "Your food will get cold, Ellen darling. You are dreaming again!"

Dream. Perhaps we both dreamed, mother and I, though differently. She may have dreamed back into her childhood, full of quiet days, where there were no Christian feasts or strange church tracts. Now she may have felt tormented and mentally oppressed. People had tried to give her the wings of Christianity; they had been pinned on her. But they hung down lifelessly. They were too heavy. They pulled her to the ground. She was unable to lift herself with them.

In the eyes of the strict Dr. med. Burchard, the Jewish woman his eldest son intended to marry may have resembled the statue of the "Synagogue" on the Strassburg cathedral. There her personification stands blindfolded, lean, bent slightly to the side, not realizing that the lance she holds is broken. Mother's eyes also seemed blindfolded. Under the pressure of the old gentleman, my dear mother converted from her liberal Jewish faith, which she had been used to in the Warburg home since her youth, to the strange Christian creed and began her married life as a Christian.

But Gertrud, the eldest child of this marriage, later sneaked into the library, picked up the crumpled tracts from the waste-basket, and hid them under her mattress. In the evening they were carefully smoothed out and read. Their contents were much easier to understand than the words in her schoolbook for religious instruction, but the pictures they contained were never as beautiful as those in Granny's large Doré Bibles.

I once heard the cook say there was no Christian spirit in our house. On the other hand, Christian methods of threatening and punishment were used to educate the children, the old spinster stated. How could a child grow up and become adult without God, without the devil and hell? We were threatened with "the black man"; we thought he was the chimney sweep. Then there was Father Christmas, who stood before us with beard and stick. We were terribly afraid of him. But my brothers soon found that father had played him. When the door bell rang, I felt rather frightened, but my brothers made sarcastic remarks: "Well, let's see what nonsense the old man is going to offer us this year!" There were many variations for father in this game, and they were always charming.

The religious instruction in school was in the hands of one of Hamburg's leading ministers, and this, plus the kind and under-standing instruction of our governesses, created a strong religious inclination in me. Though my family smiled, I began my

Christian path alone. In 1922 at the age of sixteen I was confirmed in the small St. Johanniskirche in Eppendorf, where Pastor Heitmann gave me a confirmation verse: "And now abideth faith, hope, charity, these three; but the greatest of these is charity" (1 Corinthians 13:13).

After my confirmation, Christmas had a Christian meaning for me; it became a festive ceremony. I walked the long way from home to the little Eppendorf church alone, humming Christmas carols. The small church was lighted and decorated festively. Although the place was overcrowded and warm, the atmosphere created by the carols and the organ tied us all together. It was just wonderful!

I was never in a hurry to get home. Snow lay on the streets. I was all alone, and sometimes I looked back at my own footsteps in the snow, a happy young creature in a new white land.

Because of my dawdling, I was not pleasantly welcomed at home after my "Christian escapade." The cook groaned, "How late you are, Miss Gertrud! The carp falls off its bones and the goose got dark golden meanwhile! I wonder what the master will say." The master said nothing. He took his Gertrud into his arms and pressed her against his chest. He may have felt the same when young, and so he understood.

Now all that belonged to Christmas passed only too fast: the dinner with carp and goose; the distribution of the Christmas gifts; then the beautiful tree and the multitude of parcels opened, with contents that fulfilled secret wishes; the reverence of the maids, who expressed thanks for the linen they received for their dowry. *And* the dreadful vomiting of the dachshund, who had overeaten once again!

On the evening of the second festive day, we all reached the lowest point of all under father's command: "All members of the house community have to line up by height! Castor oil will be taken. There is only one choice: either in coffee or in lemon juice!"

Because this procedure was repeated every Christmas, nobody objected. Also, father, as the last victim, very demonstratively used to swallow a big spoonful himself. Only the dachshund loved the castor oil. He licked his little plate until it was quite shiny.

Mother stood aside, sad and dreamy. She made work for herself in other rooms, something I could not understand. Once I found her crying on her bed and I asked her if she had a pain. She only shook her head and went on crying. But then she proudly threw back her head, blew her nose as though her sorrow were at an end, and said kindly, but in a rather harsh voice, "I am so glad for you, Gertrud, that you can be so enthusiastic about all this. I have been forced into it, and that does not work!"

"And why have you been forced, Mum dear?"

"Because I love Dad so much that I accepted Grandfather Burchard forcing me into Christianity. He did not want a mixed marriage!"

A word I had never heard before, a conception the meaning of which I did not understand. I did not want to ask my mother, who looked so sad and tired. But I remembered the word. It seemed to be fixed into my brain.

After comforting my mother, I sneaked into the library and got the encyclopedia from the shelf, looking for information. I found it: *"Mixed marriage*—marriage between members of different creeds or races." There it was in black and white: two people of different creeds who got married made a "mixed marriage." I was not interested in what was called "races," for to me they were Chinese, Negroes, or Indians.

But what was there to cry about? Was a "mixed marriage" something bad or dishonorable? Mother must have had deep reasons to cry on a festive day! The question was not answered. It tormented me.

But it was not only the problem of the mixed marriage that I was thinking about. I also tried to trace another one, because everything has a beginning, I told myself. It was the same in the Bible, and in those years I tried to read the Book of All Books from beginning to end. I well remember my impression of the passage in Genesis 3:7: "And the eyes of them both were opened and they knew that they were naked. . . ."

How often I asked myself how it all began. I retraced the path of my childhood to find the beginning, when it was that my eyes had been opened to know: my Warburg grandparents were Jews. And as often as I have retraced the path of memories, I do not know it. Really, I do not know.

School and secondary school were finished, followed by a year as a teacher in England, at the first coeducational school in Great Britain, where I worked as a teacher of German at Bedales School, Petersfield, Hants. This left many impressions. Then my studies in natural science at the University of Hamburg began. In these years of hard and intensive work, I left the Feldbrunnenstrasse early to hear as many lectures as possible and to attend as many seminars as I could fit in. I took sandwiches and fruit with me, to save money. When I came home at night, I was very tired indeed.

Botany and zoology, chemistry and physics, geography and ethnology were vast fields to cope with, and during the evening meals I quietly followed my own thoughts. Then I went up to my room on the second floor of the house, to work, to revise the notes I had taken during the lectures of the day, to underline scientific words with different colored pencils. I was an eager and industrious student. I worked so hard that I was not able to make friends among my fellow students. I wanted to finish my studies as soon as possible. I wanted to earn money and free my parents from all costs for me.

A young person who grows up in a large port like Hamburg constantly smells water, the sea, tar, and seaweed. There, for me, the wind created exciting noises when it blew through the rigging of ships. Thus, geography and ethnology understandably stirred a great resonance in my heart. Lectures and seminars in the Institute for Geography, Rothenbaum-Chaussee, fascinated me especially. I learned about Oriental societies and their dependence on the nature of their countries. I also studied the influence of geographical factors on human beings.

Then, quite alone, in the midst of absolutely strange people, I encountered another word. It was spoken in a lecture, one such as young people eagerly follow, trying to memorize as much as possible. A word was spoken, harshly pronounced and spun out—one that was later used as a vicious propaganda weapon—a word whose misuse shattered and besmirched our century—the word: RACE.

That day, when I encountered the word in this sense for the first time, we listened to a lecture about Hamites and Semites, descendants of Noah and in the Old Testament known as Ham and Sem. In connection with these old, well-known stories I heard the professor make a remark, a remark made with a lifted voice. It sounded like a prophecy: "No matter where they go, the Jews of these days are Semites. The Jews belong to this damned race—and this race is the misfortune of all of us!"

There it was. There it was clearly spoken in the connection: JEW—RACE. And in the emphasis, in the *way* it was spoken, I found such a great threat!

This happened at the beginning of 1928. I felt so lonely. Once again I was the only girl among unfamiliar students. I did not know what to do. I felt miserable. Then I thought about Granny. I closed my eyes.

In the row behind me sat a student whom I hardly knew. He had once tried to get acquainted with me, and had begun to introduce himself by telling me that his grandfather had been a doorkeeper at the W. S. Warburg Bank in Altona. When he told me this, I did not give a thought to how he might have connected my ancestors and me.

I did not like this student. He looked like a brute. He always sat behind me when we shared lectures. Now, as I sat there with closed eyes, I heard him say to a friend beside him, "That one, she's also got it. She also belongs to the wrong race. Her grandfather was the old Warburg in Altona—of course, a Jew!"

I wonder if that was meant only to be whispered. I *did* hear it. And after the horror had sunk into me, I felt like falling down a flight of stairs, in the dark. In my thoughts I hit every step, falling stiffly and painfully to the bottom. When, in my thoughts, I got up again, I felt bruised and destroyed. And this feeling stayed. Till today.

The lecture came to an end; it was the last of the day. It was time to go home, but I could not. I slowly strolled to the Alster lake. I sat on a bench for a long, long time and looked out over the water. I thought of what I had heard. I tried to collect my thoughts. I was certain that father would notice my consternation and ask what had caused it.

Among the memories that suddenly crossed my mind again was the imposing picture of St. Peter's Cathedral in Rome, which Granny had so wonderfully built up for my brother Albert and me: the building itself, a church concert in the wonderful nave, and in the end the consecration of two American bishops by the Pope himself. One of them was a black man— to the white men a member of a different race. And this black man received the highest honor without dispute, as pleasing to God. A different race, like the Jews, as I was once told. And his skin was black; I felt this was strange to me. And the crowd in St. Peter's hailed the black man, and all this happened in the eyes of the Lord. And I was certain that, among all of them, there was nobody who would have whispered, "That one, he also has got it!"

No, it did not touch the black man.

But I, I had "got it"———had "got it."

It may have been one of those unknown, secret blessings, that I could not get a zoological thesis for work toward my doctoral degree. Holiday work at the bird-watching stations of Helgoland and Rossitten, where I earned some money to finance my studies, had stimulated my interest in ornithology, and the migration of birds was one of those items in science that fascinated me greatly.

Instead of this I ended up in a totally different branch of science by chance. While I was working with a microscope in a seminar of old Professor Dr. H. Klebahn, looking at tiny fungi, he asked me if I was prepared to take up a special project in his laboratory, since he could not get to it. It was very much on his mind, he said. I accepted at once, not knowing why. It must have been an act of instinct.

They were wonderful years in the vast laboratory under the roof of the Institute for Botany, with its mansard windows. I worked under the guidance of the old gentleman, who had such a wonderful sense of humor. I had a key to the Botanical Gardens as well as to the institute. I was there so far away from the world, rapt in science, that I recovered from the shock.

At the end of 1928, I finished my thesis to the satisfaction of Professor Klebahn. He gave it the title "Contribution to the Knowledge of Parasite Fungi." In November 1928, I passed the oral examination with honors and had my thesis printed free of charge in a botanical journal, which was a great financial help. Granny and Grandfather Burchard were very impressed by the fact that I had become a Doctor of Natural Science. To me this meant the end of an apprenticeship and the beginning of life as an adult in a learned profession.

But the German world of my childhood had changed drastically during my studies. There was hardly any talk anymore at home, either at table or otherwise. Every member of the family was occupied with his own observations and kept them to himself. But we all noticed changes in the street: Marching groups with red Swastika flags. Children in brown uniforms, and gentlemen who, when they met, greeted each other by jerkily lifting their outstretched right arms. I even knew some of them.

The word "ARYAN" appeared in large letters on posters. Its definition, as given in press propaganda, differed greatly from the one I had heard in the university lectures. There, "Aryan" was a linguistic term. I consulted father's encyclopedia. To my astonishment, I found that the concept "Aryan," which I had learned correctly had been shattered to fit an anti-semitic doctrine. The German "Aryan" was set against the alien species of "non-Aryan." The German "Aryan"? All I had learned fought against the false antithesis that there were "non-Aryans" in contrast to "Aryans"! I discovered that we children of a "mixed marriage" were supposedly not "Aryans," but "non-Aryans"; we were said to be of "mixed breed."

In the years to follow, laws were established on the basis of this unreal distinction, which sprang from the sick brains of the Nazis, setting up cruel discrimination against all of us as a family. In my imagination the symbol for a paragraph took on a human shape. It had a central body with a bent limb, which carried a head. The other limb bent down and could move on one foot. Such figures represented all the new regulations assembled in a dense circle. They seemed to dance around us. Their heads became incandescent, and they followed everybody who tried to escape, shooting flames, so that nobody could get out.

But where was the border between this constantly persecuting imagination and reality? Again and again items with a fixed meaning were twisted and distorted. As a scientist, I had learned that the crossbreeding of animals and plants followed the rules of Mendel and that such crossbreeding had positive results. But now, suddenly, all scientific perception stopped before the crown of creation, before the human being. There everything was suddenly totally different.

Mixture and mixed marriages were condemned. Only pure races had importance, and among these the blue-eyed blond people were extolled: the German-"Aryan" people, "good for breeding." I knew that the real Aryans came from warm areas, where people were dark-eyed and dark-skinned. It was absolutely senseless to think at all or to try to follow these questions logically. Where was the world I had been born into, which I had acquired myself; where was it?

We all sat at table, a nearly classic example of Mendelian laws. There was our blue-eyed father, with his magnificently bald head. His eldest son, Albert, inherited the blue eyes. There was our mother with her beautiful brown eyes and her dark hair, which fell in long wide waves, which she handed down to my younger brother Oswald and to me. As youngest of us four children, our junior sister, Marie, inherited light gray eyes and blondish hair. But certainly the blue-eyed members of our family were not "Aryans"!

We all realized this in 1929, and we also knew how much we were caught in the entanglement of this period, without yet knowing that the thread spun would be knotted to a net, from which there would be no escape.

In the same year I left Hamburg to work at the University of Bonn. The old university city, the connection with unknown people, and last but not least what I considered a large amount of self-earned money—absorbed me. Besides my own laboratory work and my duties in the experimental areas, I had been asked to assist in the preparation of a doctoral thesis. The institute was called the "Pastor School," because the director and nine of his students were ministers' sons from the country. The fathers had made the familiar social ascent from farmer to teacher to minister, and the sons intended to acquire the esteemed title of Dr. Agr., Doctor of Agriculture. To achieve this goal they all had to get their agricultural diplomas first. All my students were at least four years my senior. It was an harmonious and sociable group of young men, who sometimes interrupted their scientific work by singing contrapuntal hymns.

In this house of men—with the exception of a secretary and a woman photographer—I arrived as a new Doctor of Science and aroused curiosity and interest. The director's assistants were an entomologist and a phytopathologist. I had no working connection with either of them. I knew that they both met at the same time in the photographic laboratory, but that was no concern of mine.

Then one day I had to have some specimens photographed under the microscope. I carried all my material to the basement, where the darkroom and the photographic laboratory were. I knocked at the door and went in without waiting for an answer, as was the custom in the house. I had just put the microscope on the table when the phytopathologist yelled at me, "Get out! Get out as quick as you can! You don't belong here!"

The appearance of the photo lab really showed that I did not belong there. I could not see any place for scientific work.

There were long rows of Nazi propaganda leaflets, and posters hanging from the ceiling to the floor, in every size possible. It all filled the narrow place.

I returned to my private laboratory with my microscope. The reflection of the sun hurt my eyes and I closed the curtains. What would come next? Who might have found out about my "weaving defect," as father used to say? Again I seemed to be expelled. Again I felt absolutely alone.

It must have been about this time that I especially noticed one of the aspiring future doctors of agriculture, Alexander Wenzel, whom his colleagues called Wenzislav. The institute secretary had told me that he had been working on his thesis for three years but had not been able to finish it. He first caught my eye because of a terribly dirty and burned white duster he wore. I also met him in the hall, carrying flowerpots with test plants from the laboratory to the glasshouse, his thumb totally dug into the soil of the pot. His whole appearance was listless.

But soon this quiet man greeted me with special courtesy. He got me my bicycle from the shed when we all cycled to Bonn at noon to have our simple meals, which we paid for with student's tickets. In the end he asked me if we could sometimes have some cycling outings together along the Rhine, when we had afternoons off. Then one day Alexander Wenzel asked me if I would help him finish his thesis. I agreed, on the condition that he get himself a new duster. He was sorry he could not oblige, because he had made the solemn promise not to change it or even have it washed before his work was finished, and he could not alter this now, even though I had asked him to do so.

This was the situation in Bonn in 1930 when I left my work for a holiday in Hamburg. Here things were very different.

My brothers had finished secondary school and had to decide on careers. The family council, headed by Granny, gave them every liberty to choose. In her heart Granny would have loved to see one of her grandsons become a banker, because the Warburg grandparents' hopes had been shattered when their only son had died at age seven. But neither Albert nor Oswald showed any inclination for a banking career. Clearly realizing their position in a National Socialist Germany, though suffering because of the grief their decision caused the family, they emigrated between 1931 and 1933 to make a new life in South Africa and Egypt.

My junior sister also left Germany a few years later with her son, then six years old. She had been married to a teacher of the craft school where she had been a pupil, but he asked for a divorce from his "non-Aryan" wife, whose classification endangered his official position. For my mother the separation from her so beloved youngest child and her first grandchild was heartbreaking, and it was just as hard for my loving father to see this family leave for distant Australia.

Thus were the roots of an old Hamburg-Altona family, which had been so deeply implanted in German soil, damaged, wounded, and in the end torn out in the tenth generation—a family that had borne the name Warburg, as on the old tombstone, since 1668. It was the laws of the Nazi period that brought this about. The young generation left. The two older generations—Granny, her three daughters, the children of Ada M., and I—remained in Germany. Nobody spoke of the wounds. They all saw the approaching storm but stuck to their ancestral tradition, which still espoused a belief in the goodness of man.

With a heavy heart, and with a great spiritual burden, I returned to Bonn. Alexander Wenzel's quiet kindness, his persistent attachment, his commonsense way of looking at things, surrounded me again, like a cloak. Mutual theatergoing, excursions into the Siebengebirge, outings along the Rhine on our bicycles gave us two lonely ones the chance to exchange ideas. And on a beautiful afternoon, when we descended on foot from the Drachenfels to Rhöndorf, Alex asked me very timidly— frightened about his own courage—if I would marry him. My startled response to this unexpected question must have confused him deeply. I just could not answer. I was thinking, What does he know about me?

Then for the first time, his arm slid under mine, and he said, "A bit farther on there is a bench, with a beautiful view over the Rhine. Let's sit down there and talk it all over."

And there, on that bench with the magnificent view over Nonnenwerth, I told Alex of my Jewish mother, and how I loved her. Only that.

"Nobody has chosen his parents," said Alex. "Me neither. And it's not up to us to judge such things. What's starting to happen these days seems to me to be presumptuousness, which will not come to a good end."

It was this answer that made me place my hand in his and give him the answer he was hoping for. We decided not to talk about this new development in the institute, but to work hard together, so that he could finish his thesis. After that we intended to leave Bonn at the same time, to make our new life. But, above all, our families had to be informed about our decision.

Alexander Wenzel came from the Taunus and was the second son of a minister who had died before my arrival in Bonn. His mother, who came from the lower nobility and who lived in Bad Homburg vor der Höhe, tried hard to hide her disappointment at the prospect of a "non-Aryan" daughter-in-law. Already in 1931 she had decorated her house with a Swastika flag when the Nazis called for it.

My family, who had feared that I would finish my life as a scientific bluestocking behind a microscope, accepted the young doctor of agriculture kindly, because he was going to lead the last Burchard child toward a normal future.

Alex had hoped that an aunt of his would lease him a farm she owned. But she did not, because she did not want her favorite nephew (she had no children of her own) to marry an educated woman. It was now up to us to build something on our own.

At the beginning of 1931, we went to different poultry farms for instruction. We learned from the beginning: cleaning manure from sheds, mixing feed, plucking feathers, attending to the incubators. The last two months of a year's training we spent together in the home of a pensioned police sergeant. The first night after our arrival, he took us to a fireman's ball. He sat behind a huge beer keg and enjoyed himself tremendously when old and young people waltzed past him.

Suddenly the old sergeant started to hoot loudly, while slapping his thighs. Two huge women danced past, holding each other tightly. "Do you see those two? They are our best battle horses! They are the cloakroom and toilet room attendants. Now it is time for father also to have a dance!" We followed him.

In autumn of 1931 we thought we knew enough about poultry, beginning in the egg and ending in the soup. We felt able to start a poultry farm of our own. In October 1931 we got married in Hamburg. The officer at the registry enjoyed a rare pleasure: the young couple and both their witnesses, all four of them, had doctoral degrees! Pastor Heitmann, who had celebrated my confirmation gave us the same confirmation verse on our marital way. A festive dinner was held in my parents' house at Feldbrunnenstrasse No. 21, which was decorated with all that was traditional and beautiful conjured from an old family's boxes and trunks. This finished a wonderful day.

In 1931 we moved into our own house, built near the Osterholz forest in Gruiten. Our present was happy and "swinging," but the future hung like a dark cloud over our low red-tiled roof.

7

Torn Roots

The small community of Gruiten with its frame houses surrounds the two small churches in the valley. Only a few cottages follow the narrow creek. Encircled by weeping willows, enlivened by happy fowl cackling, the air filled with the scent of freshly baked bread from several local bakeries, crossed by a narrow road, Gruiten seemed to be a fairy-tale village.

The roofs of the old houses in the Bergisch-Land were covered with slate slabs. Often the weather-side walls were also covered with slate, looking gray and drab, making the buildings seem a sad and insignificant cluster of huts. But from the sunny side these villages looked bright and happy, their walls whitewashed between the dark framework. The window shutters were painted bright green. There were colorful flower boxes along the fronts of the houses, and most doors, painted rust red, seemed inviting.

Up the hill, about two miles from the village of Gruiten, industrial enterprises built up another Gruiten near the railway station. There were factories, large storehouses, flat buildings, and shops, and, in the center, like a hen with her brood, visible everywhere, the red-brick village hall, large and showing off.

Gruiten belonged to the rural district of Düsseldorf-Mettmann and the administrative district of Düsseldorf. The small place could be found on nearly all maps, because it was important for all railway lines across Germany. Nearly all trains from the north and east passed Wuppertal and then reached the Gruiten junction, where they went either to Köln or Düsseldorf. This twelve-track railway line was one of the busiest in Germany and passed about a hundred and fifty yards from our house. We knew the big international trains and the times they passed by. Often we stood on the large lawn before the house and waved to friends, whom we could make out at their compartment window when the train whizzed past.

Our house, a few miles from the village of Gruiten and the railway station, was built to fit into the landscape. It was white-washed, had wooden balconies and green shutters, and was a two-story structure with a completely finished attic, whose windows looked like eyes peering out of the large, low-reaching red roof. This extremely large roof was aggressively red in 1931, but soon moss from the forest settled between the roof tiles, and in time every shade and variation of red and green could be found. The large roof rested like a hood on the house and gave it an air of security.

The slope of the countryside started at the railway tracks and fell toward the Kleine Düssel creek, behind which it mounted again into the Osterholz, a forest in which old beeches were rooted on chalk rocks. The huge beeches on the rim of this forest were so old that they may have given shelter under their low-hanging branches to the retreating army of Napoleon, who came this way.

Alex and I moved into this quiet landscape and carried with us all the hopes and plans that every young couple take into a new home of their own. The building of a poultry farm, the erection of the fowl sheds, the planting of fruit trees, the placing of incubators—it all filled the first winter in Gruiten. The eight acres of land that belonged to the poultry farm were fenced in by a strong mesh fence, six feet high. The area had been taken from a farm called Birschels, which belonged to Alex's family and was leased. In spring the neighboring farmer came with his plow and three horses. He plowed long furrows where I had planned the vegetable garden and left me with the battle against weeds and couch grass. Then we bought some young hens, and it was not long before eggs for sale showed the good sense of this new enterprise.

In addition to all this new way of living, my own household, family visitors, and the beginning of a relationship with the neighbors gave me much pleasure. The daily routine and the tremendous demand of physical work, which I was not used to, made me sleep as deeply as any farmhand. And so we slid sleeping and content into a new year.

The visit of a neighbor suddenly woke me up out of all my happy dreams. He was the senior son of the farm next door, a farmer himself, a gentlemen's race rider, and a friendly and pleasant fellow with whom Alex often talked about the area's agricultural problems, because he had spent all his life near the Osterholz. One night he came to inquire about something, so he said, when Alex opened the door.

Before sitting in the offered chair, he asked, "Listen, doctor, I know you own such a thick genealogical tome with a tremendous number of names. May I have a look at it, please?"

I readily handed him the large volume, which had its place at the bottom of the bookcase. It was the family tree of the Samsons, the family of my grandfather Albert Warburg's mother. The book had last been printed in 1912. The neighbor looked over the names in alphabetical order, 2,500, of them, and found the one of the person he was looking for.

Happily he closed the genealogy, slapped his thighs with pleasure, and remarked, "Well, didn't I think so at once? I recently met somebody at a tournament of the SS brigade who looked funny to me and with a drunken head I said to him, 'Well, comrade, you too don't look quite Aryan!' You should have seen him blush! Of course, he started to argue and deny everything, and he also constantly pointed to the magnificent insignia on his uniform collar and then said that he would sue me for libel. I left to avoid a brawl and said to myself, 'Well,

I shall see if I find that guy in the family tree of our doctor—and then I shall finish him off!' "

The neighbor rose and wanted to leave. He had achieved his purpose. I did not let him go before he had promised me, on his word of honor, that he would leave that man in peace.

"All right," the neighbor called out, rather amused. "I do hope you yourself have the two Aryan grandmothers. You will soon need them!"

Me? I myself? Who might be interested in something like that, here among fowls and old beech trees? I had long known that two of my four grandparents, the Warburgs, were Jews. And with this fact I also knew that two "Aryans" were missing.

The same evening, while Alex smoked his cigar and read his newspaper, I said farewell to my family tree. I leafed through the descendants of Marcus Gumpel Moses Fulda, who immigrated to Fulda and obtained his letter of safe-conduct there on April 15, 1697. Some of his descendants donated money for the foundation of the "Samson Legatenfund" in 1786, which supplied finances for a school and for family research. In this connection the last genealogy was printed in an authorized publication and sent to all members of the family. Granny had given me her copy. Eight generations were lined up in large registers. Eight generations, approximately 2,500 people.

For a whole evening my thoughts were absorbed by the document, from which the development of a period could be seen. Besides many artists and intellectuals, it was astonishing how many noblemen from internationally well-known families and how many officers married into the Jewish families. Certainly many of their daughters may have been touchingly beautiful and full of charm, but probably the "movement" may have attracted many of them also—the movement that really means something in the world and makes it turn—the movement of counting money between thumb and forefinger. Often young officers had to make high deposits, to get into the active service of royal regiments—and where to take them from?

At the end of the eighth generation it was not difficult to detect that not even a quarter of the descendants of the Wolfenbüttler ancestors were "pure Jews." But it was more than frightening in 1932, when I said farewell to my family tree, which listed 2,500 people whose descendants were still alive, but for those who had recently married into the family, nobody was "purely Aryan"!

Realizing the danger that the book represented, I packed it into a watertight box and buried it the same night, under the peat shed, using a carbide lamp to find my way. After carefully smoothing the soil, I felt hollow and lonely. I felt as if I had buried a piece of myself.

The horror approached. The danger became more and more visible. The disaster, which might have already caught up with me, still seemed very far away. The outcome of the election in November of 1932 cruelly pulled away the thin veil that had hung before my soul. On January 30, 1933, Adolf Hitler became Chancellor of Germany. The Nazis had come to power.

With my first child under my heart I tried to cope with the coming difficulties, using my brain. The blood of the Warburgs also pulsed in the veins of the unborn, and I had to try to keep this, *my* child, from being stamped as a person of inferior value, a pariah. Every slur on his personality as being "different" would expel him from the community of equal and strong ones, who would always have stones, sticks, and scornful laughter ready for him. As an animal fights for its young, I was determined to defend my child!

This determination to fight resulted in many, many letters. Registered letters with return postage went to all registration offices and church registers, to Breslau, where my father came from, inquiring about all dates. So as not to attract attention in Gruiten, I posted all letters in Wuppertal and received the answers at a postal box there.

The numerous officials were not yet overworked by the demands for such papers from people who were chasing after their "Aryan" ancestors. They answered quickly and kindly. So I was able to state, by showing officially stamped papers and documents, that all Burchard ancestors down to my father's grandparents, my great-grandparents, had been baptized:

1. *My Grandfather Burchard:*
San. Rat. Dr. med. Albert August Burchard, born February 10, 1845, son of Dr. med. Leopold Burchard, Protestant, and his wife, Berta née Krause, Protestant, baptized Apr. 6, 1845, in the Protestant church of Saint Maria Magdalena in Breslau.

2. *My Grandmother Burchard:*
Anna Maria Auguste Hermine Windmüller, born July 28, 1858, daughter of Dr. iur. Friedrich Wilhelm Eduard Windmüller, Royal solicitor and notary, Protestant, and his wife, Berta née Friedlander, Protestant, baptized in the Protestant church of St. Bernardin, October 20, 1850, in Breslau.

3. *My Father:*
Dr. iur. Edgar Eduard Walter Burchard, son of (1) and (2), born July 6, 1879, baptized September 14, 1879, in the Reformed Church in Breslau.

These documents proved that my father was an "Aryan" by ancestry. However, counting as the Hitlerites did, it worked out as follows:

    2 "Aryan" grandparents Burchard   = 1 "Aryan" father
    2 Jewish grandparents Warburg   = 1 Jewish mother
            By this equation, I was   = "Half-Jewess."

Although all of Alex's ancestors were "pure Aryans," the beloved unborn child I was carrying had an "Aryan" father and a "half-Jewish" mother. In the Nazi classification, he would be a "quarter-Jew." There was absolutely no way to deny it.

While I was gathering papers in Gruiten, the "Aryan" regulation, though not yet legal, began to hit our Hamburg family hard. As mentioned, one of my brothers had already emigrated, and my second brother and my sister were working on their papers so as to leave Germany forever.

In this extremely depressing time our son was born, on Granny's seventy-sixth birthday. With the happiness of the appearance of a new life in the family—and above all because it was a boy—hardly anybody noticed that this child appeared at a time when Hitlerism was becoming entrenched in Germany.

We had decided to call our son Oscar, because we liked this name. There had never been an Oscar in the family and nobody would be offended. So Alex went to the registry to report the birth of his son. Some books were consulted and it was found that *Oscar* with a *c* was not permitted; it was "not German." Oskar was registered with a *k* and was thus a child with a German name. As a German with a German name, the little boy was just one week old when the Nazi Party was declared the sole political party in Germany.

All civil service officials and functionaries had to prove their "Aryan" descent. My father's family had only one public official, his brother Dr. iur. Oswald Burchard, two years his junior. He had to hand in his papers as a judge to the Hamburg Legal Department and declare himself under the Nürnberg Laws as "mongrel in the first grade." He died as a judge in office on October 11, 1940.

The classification of my father's brother as a "half-Jew" changed my parents' position suddenly and hopelessly. Because of the Nazi racial regulation a "half-Jew" like my father, married to a "pure Jewess" like my mother, had additional Jewish ties and was now counted as a "FULL—Pure—Jew"! From the moment that my parents understood this Hitlerite classification, they knew that every anti-Semitic action would hit them full blast.

Because of the statement that my uncle had given and because of the changed position of my parents, my position also changed drastically. I now officially had a "half-Jewish" father and a Jewish mother in Hamburg, and so I was mathematically a "three-quarter Jewess" myself. In the Hitlerite classification, every fraction above a half was rounded off, and so I was made a "Jewess" and my little Oskar a "half-Jew."

Hamburg was far away. The letter in which my father told me of these gruesome facts arrived when Alex was not at home. I did not show him the letter. He never saw it. I did not want to burden him with this knowledge. I thought that this was *my* responsibility only. In a return letter to father, I asked him to inform the family that only I knew about this Sword of Damocles and would not take any action whatever regarding myself. I stressed that Alex did not know anything about it at all.

When the forms regarding ancestral questions arrived in Gruiten, and every German had to answer to the questions asked, I handed in all documents down to the baptism of my grandparents Burchard-Windmüller and described myself as a "half-Jewess." This happened in 1935, after the Reichstag had agreed in Nürnberg, on September 15, 1935, to the Racial Laws "to protect the German race." The laws had been ratified in the same year that a unity of state and party had been created. Thus the state was handed over to the Nazi Party.

And we were handed over too.

Dates from My Family Tree
(Hitler Fashion, 1935)

BURCHARD, Albert August,
               Dr. med.
    b. 10.2.1845 in Breslau
    d. 16.8.1932 in Hamburg

WARBURG, Albert, Kom. Rat.
    b. 23.6.1843 in Altona
    d. 20.2.1919 in Hamburg

WINDMÜLLER, Anna Maria
           Auguste Hermine
    b. 18.7.1850 in Breslau
    d. 26.11.1926 in Hamburg

RINDSKOPF, Gertrude Mar-
          garetha (Gerta)
    b. 23.11.1856 in
          Amsterdam

BURCHARD, Edgar Eduard
          Walter, Dr.iur.
    b. 6.7.1879 in Breslau

WARBURG, Helene Julie (Ellen)
    b. 10.9.1877 in Altona

BURCHARD, Gertrud Anna, Dr.rer.nat.,
             marr. Wenzel
b. 2.3.1906 in Kiel.

        ✝ = non-Jew
        ✡ = Jew
        △ = Half-Jew
        ▽△= Three-quarter Jew

8

In the Trap of the Paragraphs

In 1934 Granny wrote me a letter. That was long ago, but the letter is still beside me:

> Dear Gertrud, you were right to tell me about it all. For a long time Betty and I have separated our estates for tax reasons. I believed in Russia and have believed since 1917 that Lenin would be victorious after the last world war, because it was only he who had an idea which knows no borders. I never thought of the way it all happened. I never would have thought it possible. Also today I do not believe that in the long run it will be possible to fight races and freedom and belief. It would be a poor show for a great and intelligent nation. Then the French Revolution would have been in vain. I am glad that your brothers went to foreign countries. Whether they will succeed seems very doubtful to me, but at least they do not live as pariahs.
>
> Of course, it is all difficult for Oskar's education, but I believe that baptism has to be a sacrament, then your parents and yourself are Christians. If it is not looked upon as such, who, then, are Christians? One should be a good and decent human being; then it would not matter into which creed our ancestors were born. After all it is just a question of power. Children grow into their time. They will find theirs just as beautiful as all children, should they later think differently than their contemporaries. They will become happy or unhappy because of their temperaments. All important people

are ahead of their time. They are human beings, not just people. They do not belong to a collective, but to rule over the latter is easier. That may be the reason for the change. The masses want to adore something, and that now seems to be a leader. Enough of philosophy for now!

Be happy and do not save too much; they will take it all away again. Enjoy the beauty of nature, the wonderful springtime; that is the most beautiful of all. Nature may change at time with the seasons, but never so much that it will not stay beautiful and an everlasting possession.

Tomorrow the daughter of my old friend C. H. gets married without any fuss. Perhaps it will bring happiness. It is said that marriages are made in heaven. I wonder if they know "non-Aryans" up there.

Well, miserable times, but my health improves. I am fatalistic and optimistic, or indifferent; it all seems to be the same. Communism is only a transition. "All flows" was what the ancient Greek said. Alex may tell you this in Greek. I can only read it, but not write it.

A thousand greetings!

G.

There is another passage in a letter from the same year:

Once in life everybody has his good time. A good time to my way of thinking is one in which the human being develops, in which he is esteemed, and in which he is happy. But, Gertrud, I would like you to know that one can make good times oneself: one has to manage oneself!

I thought that Granny had certainly had many "good times," because she had managed to cope with everything.

———

In 1935 new difficulties arose. The bank papers, the interest on which had paid for the Hochallee household, dropped further. Even our humble standard could not be kept up. Even after the first alteration of the house, which gave Aunt Betty the chance to have her medical practice on the ground floor, the house was still too spacious. Granny, looking for another source of income, decided to rent rooms herself.

The constantly changing building codes of 1935 were very frightening to the old lady. Both her sons-in-law offered to help, but she rejected all offers. In her tremendous persistence she took up the battle with the building officials, and won, at the age of seventy-eight! She got permission for alterations. The ground floor was changed into two small separated apartments, which were very nice and easily found tenants. Granny sold her Steinway grand piano, on which so many well-known musicians had played. With the same graciousness, she said farewell to the large open fireplace of her spacious lounge, making the remark she always used when such problems arose: "Good to have gotten rid of some ballast again!"

Granny and Aunt Betty had two rooms each on the first floor of the house, and my aunt set up her office there. There was also a tiny kitchen, where Aunt Betty attended to the cooking with "surgical" precision. Despite difficulties, Granny was full of praise for her daughter-cook!

Granny's rooms looked to the Hochallee. Aunt Betty's opened to the garden toward the Parkallee. There I found her one day sitting with clasped hands. Her eyes blinded by tears, she looked into the garden. On her sewing table was an open letter. She said I should read it. It officially declared that Jews were no longer allowed to have patients who were members of the Medical Health Plan.

There this lovable, kind, and devoted aging woman sat like a tormented animal from whom a cynical hand had cut the nerve of life. She became a cripple. So as not to worry Granny she would talk for hours with her canary about all that occupied her mind and soul. She looked after her flower boxes more busily than ever and eagerly waited for the bell to ring and bring her some patients. But only family members came in the daytime, and sometimes after dark some former patients, who wanted the help of "their" doctor.

There were always bunches of flowers on her desk, gifts from grateful poor people whom she had treated free of charge. They had placed them at her door anonymously, in the dark. But the charmingly happy, all-knowing smile of this woman, who was willing to help suffering humanity as a medical practitioner, withdrew forever from her face. The cruel racial laws, which had taken away her basic interest in helping the poor, led to deep lines around the corners of her mouth. Only small children, and above all her deeply beloved grandnephew Oskar Wenzel, could bring all her old charm back into her face.

After reading Granny's letter, in which she told me that the alterations to the house were finished, I decided in mid-November 1935 to visit my family in Hamburg. Work on the farm had gotten done, so I could take a vacation. Alex drove us to the train at Wuppertal and put us in a second-class compartment. The only other passenger was a woman who occupied a seat by the window. Oskar, nearly two, was very excited and enthusiastic and waved happily to his father as the train pulled out. It was his first train trip.

The lady opposite me was very blonded up and read the *Stürmer,* a rabid Hitlerite paper. Oskar, of course, did not notice anything and had a small toy train running from my knees over the seats on our side to the corridor and back. He was very busy and completely occupied.

Suddenly the lady addressed me: "You really have a charming little boy, madam, and how typically Aryan he is! I've been looking at him for some time. *That's* the kind of child that Hitler wants! And he has such a perfect Nordic skull! Wonderful indeed!"

She grabbed Oskar. He started to yell tremendously while she measured his head with her outstretched hand: "Correct, absolutely correct measurements. Wonderful indeed!"

She put Oskar down, gave him a lollipop from her handbag, and began to read the *Stürmer* again. When she left the train at Hagen, she gave a fierce Nazi salute and rasped, "Heil Hitler!"

A youngish gentleman with a golden Party insignia entered our compartment and made friends with Oskar at once. The child seemed to like the shiny golden decoration in the gentleman's buttonhole. The man took it out and gave it to Oskar. The boy dropped it, and it rolled under the seats on our side. I was distressed, but the gentleman simply picked it up and put it in his pocket.

"I have the feeling, madam," he said, "that you like me better without the decoration." He tried to begin a conversation. I didn't say anything, but listened with interest. The gentleman told me his name and said he was the junior son. His father had owned a large country estate, which had been left to the eldest child, his brother. He was now a member of the Reichsbauern-gericht (farmers court) in Goslar. Because the family farm had gone to his brother, he had been one of the discontented who had early joined the Nazi Party and thus got the golden insignia. But now neither their goals nor their politics in general interested him. He stuck to it only to get into an administrative agricultural department, which he knew something about, so he could prevent nuisances in that field. He traveled a good deal by train and always went into compartments with children, which was as entertaining as it was instructive. Although the gentleman seemed to mean well, I found the conversation rather tiring. In Bremen he left us with a friendly *"Auf Wiedersehen!"* and we stayed alone in our compartment until we reached Hamburg.

I had planned the trip to Hamburg as a surprise visit on Granny's seventy-eighth birthday, which was also Oskar's second birthday. We took a taxi to the Hochallee and passed the front garden. I opened the outside door and put my suitcase down, but I still had my little son on my arm. When I stretched my hand out to ring the bell, I was struck motionless by a sight on the wall of the entrance, which had been altered with the house: a Dutch flag was draped in large folds around a framed document, which showed a huge red seal. The sight really jumped at me! The Dutch Consulate in Hamburg confirmed that the widow of Albert Warburg, Gertrude Margaretha, née Rindskopf, born November 23, 1856, in Amsterdam, was of Dutch nationality. I realized that Granny had put up this document as a security measure.

After breathing heavily a few times to avoid crying, I rang the bell. Granny herself came down and opened the door, but only a little; the chain from the inside had not been taken off. Her astonishment when she saw us was tremendous! Silently I placed her great-grandson in her arms. She bent forward to kiss me, but suddenly stopped, looked at me just as lovingly as inquisitively, and asked, "And when is the next baby coming?"

At the time, our second child was only three months on the way. I had intended to tell Granny the great news sometime during the visit. But with the wisdom of old people she had known at once of what was going to become her future happiness.

During this visit in Hamburg, I stayed for the last time in the house of my youth, on the Feldbrunnenstrasse. I thought my mother frightfully changed, thin and nervous, also sleepless, though she took pills. She ran to the street in absolute distress when she heard the postman coming, hoping for news from her faraway sons. She was also concerned for my sister, who had gotten a divorce and would also leave soon for a faraway country, taking her little son, whom mother adored. All of this undermined her health. My father, formerly happy and lively, had become a dour old gentleman. The smile he gave Oskar looked like a crack in a frozen mask.

After two heart-warming weeks, I knew my family's attitude, which never changed: We know that humans plan inhuman actions for others, but we do *not* believe that this planning will be turned into action. Human beings cannot do this; it would mean elevating crimes to the status of law. Such crimes will be condemned by the whole world. Ethics and morality will never permit them!

My family believed in the humaneness in human nature.

Holding my little boy close, I left Hamburg in 1935, never to return.

During the following year my parents had to give up the Feldbrunnenstrasse house, because it was impossible for "non-Aryan" householders to find tenants. They moved to a nice little ground floor flat at 8 Innocentiastrasse. Soon after their move, father had a stroke, which paralyzed him on one side. He had to give up the low-paying job he had held. But he recovered rather quickly, and, when he was able to walk again, on crutches, he buckled his briefcase to his shoulder with a leather strap and eagerly attended to all the shopping for their small household. He also took the mail to the post office and was glad to be busy again.

It was a great pleasure for Granny and my parents when Alex told them, on June 24, 1936, that Oskar had a little sister. I had intended to call her Alexa, after her father. But again the list of permissible names was consulted at the registry, and Alexa was rejected. Only Alexandra was permitted, and I didn't like it. But I finally got permission from Berlin to call the little girl Alexa.

In autumn of 1936 I invited father, who was somewhat better after his stroke, to Gruiten, to see his grandchildren and enjoy the country life. He was very enthusiastic about the invitation. At the station, where I fetched him with the car, he gave me a letter from mother. He knew exactly what it said: he should keep a strict diet. Mother asked me—"Father may whine as much as he likes"—not to give him any salt or spices.

On the day of his arrival, after we had had a cup of coffee, Oskar took his grandfather's hand and said, very glibly though not yet three, "Grandpa, now I would like to show you my new sister. But you must not take her out of her basket; she is always wet. Mum told the poor little child that this was horrid. But she does not understand that yet. She is still so terribly small. And, after all, she can't help it. She is broken. She hasn't got such a thing as I have. Therefore she is always wet."

Hearing these horrid details, my father once again laughed as in olden days, and hand in hand grandfather and grandchild went up to the nursery, where they stayed for some time. Then I heard them going up to the attic, but they came down soon after.

Father complained: "Well, Tutti, since when do you lock the smokehouse? Do you intend to control me? Oskar and I were planning to try all the different kinds of sausages, cutting small pieces off with my pocketknife. Come on, give me the key!"

I pointed out that his diet would not permit such an escapade and emphasized that spiced sausages would be poison for him.

"I know, Tutti, that you have always been a good and obedient daughter and that you want to please your mother. What do I get from living a bit longer with disgusting food? I would prefer to live the life of your cockerels in their fattening stalls: beautiful and short! Come, give me the key—and, my dear, another question: Where did you put the big barrel with the salted cucumbers this year? I have to try them at once, and I can tell you they are best eaten directly from the barrel!"

I handed father the key and let him do what he liked. He was always so extremely happy in Gruiten!

Understandably, father, after returning to Hamburg, did not want to worry me with more bad news. He could have told me in Gruiten, but perhaps he guessed what Alex's reaction would be. I got the bad news from father's faithful old secretary: The money that Granny could give my parents was no longer enough to cover even their humble living standard. The old people did not want to write to me. They did not want to worry me. I had already more than enough to do, they thought. Granny herself had the courage to let me know these facts and humbly asked me to help my parents.

Her letter arrived while Alex was not home. I worked outside all day. I wanted to be alone and not see anybody. I had to think things over.

That evening Alex and I had our first argument. The worst

arguments are about money. I asked my husband for the money from what we would earn together on the poultry farm, from our joint property, or whatever. Alex rejected every suggestion and declared that, if I wanted to send money to Hamburg, I had to earn it on my own, without neglecting my present duties. Now I knew what I was up against, but my parents' need, and my pride, told me to master this task.

While I hacked at a field of turnips near the forest, quite on my own, I remembered something somebody had said about "soup cubes." There would certainly be a future in that business! I realized at once that such a product would survive hard times better than other items. I even remembered the name of the firm that produced the raw materials, and my thoughts circled more and more intensely around such a production of my own.

I still owned a bankbook from my time in Bonn as a scientific worker. It showed a balance of RM 500.11 (about $100). How well I remember the eleven pfennig! That was the only money I could handle on my own. I decided to set up my own soup-cube company.

So one day I took the car and drove to Andernach, to negotiate with the manager of the firm that was to provide me with raw materials. I had an appointment. It was late in autumn and the streets were slippery. I did not get as far as I had planned and had to spend a night with friends in Bonn, who could only put me up in their maid's room. I was terribly cold that night in the narrow iron bed. Probably additional bedding would not have warmed me, because the thought of seeing my parents starving tormented me endlessly. A further responsibility had been placed on my shoulders.

The negotiations with the junior manager of the Andernach firm were extremely pleasant and positive. Afterward I was invited to a meal in his home. There I grew confident of the couple and told them of my new plans to build my business. They may have pitied me. They may have liked me. They gave me advice and promised me all the help I needed. We became friends and still are.

What enchanted me most was their approval of my idea for

making soup cubes from fresh eggs. No such product had ever been marketed. They gave me their best wishes.

Besides this human gift, I took a large case with me back to Gruiten. It contained samples of seasonings, yeast extract, dehydrated vegetables, and herbs. I was also assured that the firm's laboratory would always be available to analyze my products.

A few days later I drove to Vohwinkel and bought a small electric stove with two hot plates and two large saucepans, as well as a kitchen scale, spoons, and various other items. I set up everything on an old garden table in an unused attic room. At night, when all my chores were done, I mounted into the well-locked little room and began to weigh, mix, and cook. Everything was carefully noted down, to avoid mistakes. I soon felt sick from the strong smell of all the ingredients—so sick that I felt I had to get some fresh air. I was already frightened of being forced to give up my new venture because of my finicky nose. I solved the problem by putting a clothespin on my nose! Then I could continue to mix, cook—and taste.

Everybody I told about my new production laughed, but everybody who tried a cup of my soup thought it was excellent. Everybody was interested in how I made it. My butcher asked, "Is there any water in it, doctor?"

I said no.

"Then there's nothing in it that's real business! Water *has* to be added! What would I do without water in my butcher shop? Every time I have a huge kettle with sausage going, I fill a big bucket with water and empty the sausage into it. Then I tell myself, 'There goes another piano lesson for Paula'—my daughter. Believe me, doctor, that's the way to get somewhere!"

The butcher wanted to see how a cup of broth was made. I put a teaspoon of my product in a cup and poured hot water on it. Then I stirred, and that was all. But, if the water was boiling, the egg that the cubes contained flaked out and became visible. It was rather easy.

In the end the tests from Andernach were satisfactory and conformed to the food regulations. My money was gone, but now the sales could begin. I earned a good deal of money, even after the investment costs had been deducted. I earned the money that my parents needed so badly. Once a month I sent some to father's old secretary, the one who had given me the distressing news. It was enough for them to get along on. The secretary would meet father in the crowd at the fish market, where she would quickly hand him an envelope with the money. The fish sellers all knew the old gentleman, who limped a bit. They gave him a discount. For each of them he had a quick-witted word, a whispered little joke, a friendly pat on the cheek. They all liked him and called him "our doctor."

No word was ever written about all this, but during this hard time father began to send weekly picture postcards to my children. The pictures showed mice, in human clothes, having many adventures. Verses were written on the cards, and, reading between the lines, I could tell what moved father's heart—and mine.

———

Press and propaganda, these new forces which can poison nations with their slogans, had roused anti-Semitism in Germany to a frenzy. Banners above the streets read "The Jews Are Our Misery." Store windows were inscribed "Jewish Shop." Restaurants, hotels, and movie houses had signs reading "Jews not wanted" or "Jews are not permitted to enter." These could be found everywhere.

According to the Nazi propagandists the Jews were the cause of all evils: unemployment, high meat prices, the cold winter, and everything else. Again and again one could read in the papers that "the soul of the people has begun to boil." And everybody could figure out for himself what would be coming one day. . . .

The human mass has always enjoyed the suffering of the defenseless, and their rage has no limit. This was true all over Germany on the night of November 9, 1938, when the synagogues were burned and Jewish property was destroyed. There were many

GERTA WARBURG, in her eightieth year

variations: A grand piano was thrown from the window of a Jewish household, to fall to pieces on the pavement, all to the great enjoyment of a yelling crowd. The big windowpanes of a Jewish shop were shattered and the display plundered. An orthodox Jew was caught and tormented by having his beard pulled. The long-aroused anti-Semitism took a dreadful toll. And the Jew, persecuted since the beginning of time, was the victim. The happenings of November 1938, when the "German soul" began to boil at the same time all over the country, entered history as a date of inhumanity—the "Reichskristallnacht."

It was during these days, when the papers wrote about all this, that somebody smashed the enamel nameplate on Granny's garden gate. The name Dr. med. Betty Warburg was shattered by a hard object. This act almost destroyed the humanitarian at Hochallee 5. But she continued to work.

Later though, after she had left an apartment where she had looked after a sick child, in the dark entrance some teenagers smashed sticks across her face. Something broke in her. Broke for good. She did not go home to the Hochallee, but fetched my father, who took her back. He told Granny, who was already worrying about Betty's absence, that she had fallen down the garden stairs on the Feldbrunnenstrasse and hurt her face badly. No word of complaint or anger ever passed Betty's lips. But still greater grief entered her beautiful gray eyes.

Granny was in her eighty-third year. She clearly observed the happenings around her, in the country, in her town, in her family, and among her acquaintances. The daily horrors did not seem to affect her, but her mouth narrowed more and more. She seemed to have moved away from all human events. She fought with herself to come to a decision, but could not reach it. She loved the German nation. She had been a part of it for sixty years. She persuaded herself that the madness of the thirties could not last. She thought it was all just one wave of insanity. She could not understand that every Swastika was a call for the destruction of the Jewish people. This woman who knew life, loved art and understood politics veiled her sight in a love for a Germany that no longer existed.

Relatives and friends who had already left Germany warned her that she should leave. They emphasized that it would be easy for her to live on the money she had in England from her dowry. She did not want to go to England. She still believed in humanity —a humanity that had long ceased to exist.

Aunt Betty was like a frightened bird. She felt like a pariah— a condition to which a fist and some sticks had brought her. She only wanted peace and could not make any decision herself. She retired into her own room more and more. Only late at night would she leave the house for a walk, armed with a stick, much too weak and frightened to use it in her defense.

My family, my parents, Granny, and Aunt Betty, were still in Hamburg when Hitler's lust for power led him to seize Bohemia and Moravia in 1939. The occupation of Austria and the German-speaking part of Czechoslovakia was profoundly disturbing and much discussed, but its full seriousness did not become clear until later.

One evening my mother called to tell me she would be coming the next day. It was only a very short call, of the kind in which unrest shows in the tone of voice, without a single word that tells of the true feeling. I went to pick her up at the train. There stood my mother. She had pulled her hat down over her face and had put up the collar of her coat. She looked like a small body of misery standing on the platform. During the drive from Elberfeld to Gruiten she did not speak a word. It was only in the easy chair near my window, with Alexa on her knees, that she at last uttered just two sentences: "Granny wants to return to Holland. Father and I have a new hope that nothing will happen to us."

Then again silence and cold horror dominated the room. The child pressed against the old woman and patted her face with her open little hand. Tears streamed down my mother's cheeks.

That same evening, when the children were in bed and Alex had gone to visit neighbors, I brewed some strong coffee for mother and myself. I thought this would help her out of her depression. Before she took her cup, she opened her handbag and handed me a closed envelope. "From father," she said. **"We don't need this anymore."**

From the envelope I took a shabby photocopy of an old document. It was difficult to read. I could barely make it out. It was strangely important and I had to breathe heavily to keep from crying.

"We don't need the document anymore," my mother repeated. "Father recently found it among his personal papers. He had totally forgotten its existence. Meanwhile father had been in Berlin, where a fellow member of his student society is now President of Hitler's personal office. This gentleman and father were friends during their joint studies. This document was photocopied in Berlin. The baptism of Grandmother Burchard's grandfather, Friedrich Wilhelm Eduard Windmüller, is confirmed in this paper. So father's Christian line continues for another generation, which means to father's grandfather. He thinks that the document should be sufficient to make him an Aryan. Father asked his friend to give him a document with the Aryan statement. If that can be managed, Gertrud, then father and I can live in a mixed marriage, with me as the Jewish part. Father is certain of his success in this case! I . . . I don't dare to think of what will happen if nothing comes of it!"

Besides the photocopy the envelope contained a small note with these words: "Perhaps this may once be of use to you, Tutti. It is the number of the document in which I apply for Aryanization: R. M. D. I. : I e Bu 23 II 40, 5017 a."

I sat very quietly and stared at the document. What could it all mean, to *me*, that His Majesty King Friedrich Wilhelm III had been the godfather to an ancestor of mine? I hid the envelope in a faraway corner of my desk and decided not to talk about it with anybody.

A few days passed. They seemed quiet, but I noticed that mother was disturbed. She longed to go home and asked me to accompany her to the train at Elberfeld. We were both very sad. It was as though she wanted to give me a last consolation when she bent out of her compartment window and said, "If all goes well, Gertrud, I shall greet you with 'Heil Hitler' when we meet again. Father is certain that his friend in Berlin is going to help him."

These were the last words I heard my mother say.

For years Jews had been forbidden to speak Hitler's name. They were also forbidden to sign letters in the Hitler fashion.

And so we passed with all our hopes—and our chains—into 1940.

9

Under the Red Roof

*May God keep man from having to suffer
all the affliction he is able to bear.*
JEWISH PROVERB

On September 1, 1939, German troops marched into Poland. This was a great shock to everyone. The Blitzkrieg in the east was not only of great political importance but also provided work for the war machine and clearly showed how the Nazis ravaged the occupied areas. We heard terrible stories: On Sundays, the churches in Poland would be surrounded by troops. After the service, every man from sixteen to sixty would be pushed onto trucks. Then special trains transported the human cargo to the German industrial centers in the Ruhr and elsewhere. The men became slave laborers in the armaments industry.

During the first days of the winter of 1940, an officer came to our house to seek quarters for soldiers of the First Army who had fought in Poland and been moved west. Most of the soldiers came from the Rhineland, the quartermaster told us. The two maids' rooms and the large guest room were commandeered. Two days later four artillery sergeants and a lieutenant moved in. Forty horses were accommodated in vacant sheds.

Until then we had had enough food, but, when the soldiers

joined us, supplies ran short. The sergeants were sick of their field-kitchen food, and my maids enjoyed serving tremendous amounts of fried potatoes to their countrymen. My argument that the food from the field kitchen could be fetched and eaten in my kitchen was derided. They brought some, but fed it to the Alsatian dogs. The men were glad to be in proper quarters again.

I was forced to lock up the food; my maids were just too softhearted toward their sergeants. The lieutenant, who had the guest room, approved my action. It was very satisfactory to have an officer in the house. Every evening at ten he opened the kitchen door and ordered the four sergeants to go to bed. If he hadn't, they never would have, because the record player had been moved to the kitchen and there was dancing every night. There was also singing with guitar accompaniment, and everybody was happy. The maids had moved into the second guest room, on the first floor.

After two weeks of this, something had to be done about our food situation. I was no longer able to feed the four sergeants and everybody else. The lieutenant got food parcels from his wife; they had a farm themselves. So I asked two of the sergeants to go on leave and get some food from their farms on the Lower-Rhine.

A few days later I heard Oskar calling me in the early morning. "Mum," he yelled through the house, "at the bottom of the refrigerator there is a whole dead pig! Come and have a look at it!"

I thought that one of the sergeants had played a joke and put a tiny marzipan piglet in our fridge, but then I realized that such luxuries had not been produced for a long time. In the end I gave in and went down, because Oskar kept pulling at me with all his strength. There really was a cleanly shaven and neatly cleaned suckling pig curled up in the fridge, the provision of one of the sergeants. Everybody agreed that the whole animal should be cooked. That was the word: roast pig and fried potatoes! That night they all helped me. Everybody had some advice, some work, and some tasting. All the containers I could lay my hands on were filled with roast pig, and every evening the favorite dish was served.

The second participant in the supply mission became very popular: he brought some sugar. In 1940 sugar too was already rationed. The soldier had filled his big fatigue jacket with sugar and tied it at the end of the sleeve. Nothing could run out. We all praised his clever move.

You could almost say we had a "happy war" in my home, because up to then the air raids had concentrated on the cities. The young people with me had no idea of the misery and destruction around us; they were just young. They enjoyed life in a private home, and all went well until both maids fell in love with the same sergeant, a dark-haired young fellow who played the guitar and had a nice voice. He sang, he turned his black eyes toward both blond sisters, and each one thought she was the favorite. Tension filled the air. The food was spoiled with salt. More porcelain was broken than usual. Both girls hoped for a war wedding, but the charmer did not marry either one. After many tears from the girls, the "East Prussians," as they were called, moved west.

More officers and soldiers moved in and out of the house. The novelty had worn off. It all now belonged to the war, which became more serious every day.

The difficulties that were put in Granny's way concerning her departure to Holland as a Dutch citizen increased constantly. She was willing to pay for Aunt Betty and herself all taxes due from Jews who intended to leave Germany, but these far surpassed her income. Again the administration of Albert Warburg's legacy permitted her to take the necessary sum. In the end Granny got permission to leave Germany with her dowry.

Granny was now eighty-three, and nearly blind from glaucoma in both eyes. She began to give away everything that would not fit in the small apartment that friends had rented for her in The Hague. Trunks and boxes were packed in the presence of the Gestapo and sealed by officials. Together with her furniture and works of art they were packed in a moving van and sealed again. By returning to Holland, Granny hoped to be able to save her heirlooms for her daughters and grandchildren. She and her dowry returned to the place they had left in 1876.

Granny and I talked on the phone once more. We discussed the future, and Granny again and again emphasized how wonderful it would be to take her great-grandchildren, my children, to Egmond aan Zee, where we had visited during our summer vacations before the First World War. We planned and planned and talked only of unimportant things. But we both certainly heard that tears were changing our voices. I still remember her last words: "Don't be impatient, my child! After all, the Thirty Years' War also came to an end!"

It was probably merciful that an operator cut off our conversation. An abrupt end and none of us had said "See you again!"

On May 8, 1940, Granny and Aunt Betty crossed the Dutch frontier. The moving van followed the same day.

On May 10, the German army crossed the same border in its advance toward Belgium and France.

Granny was not permitted to move into her apartment. The Hague was too close to the sea and too important to the German army for them to let "unreliable" people like Jews settle there. My people moved to the only city open to them, Arnheim, and settled in a humbly furnished two-room flat. The van had to stay in The Hague; its contents were put in storage.

After months of waiting, at long last I got a letter. One item stood out: "Don't worry. Now I have it as easy as my former laundress. I don't have to look after anything anymore!"

As long as the German army of occupation in Holland did not have their officials organized for a total takeover of the country, I got one letter every month. But afterward my family was watched and our mail censored. Granny began to call me "dear friend" and tried to hide our relationship. Then there were fewer letters, and in the end there was no news from Arnheim anymore.

But I heard from a soldier about the persecution of Jews in Holland. They were not permitted to visit public parks and gardens, and were chased from benches—not by the Dutch but by German control officers in plain clothes. They could go out only at fixed times, and they could buy only in certain shops. They were not permitted to write letters, read newspapers, or listen to the radio. The furniture warehouse was cleared for other purposes, and everything taken into custody disappeared into the unknown.

Soon after I heard all this, another letter from Arnheim arrived. The handwriting was poor and scrawly. It was easy to see that Granny's eyesight had gotten worse. In this letter Granny made me a present of one sentence: "Beloved friend, you'd better get used to dancing to a different tune!"

With her calmness and even temper, Granny set an example as the stronger one and supported her youngest daughter. My letters and the few photos of her great-grandchildren were her greatest pleasure. She showed them to her friends. And she had many. In their youth Granny and her sisters had been educated by a Pasteur Brun of the French-speaking Dutch Church, Église Wallonne. Once again a minister of this community took care of the two ladies: Pasteur J. F. Hayet of the Église Wallonne d'Arnheim. Members of his group tried devotedly to help all persecuted people and to ease their pains. They visited Jews without regard to possible reprisals, gave them food from their small supply, and told them news from the town. They also managed to pass on political news from the forbidden BBC, which they listened to in secret, and so helped their friends in every way possible. They even managed to get letters out of Holland without censorship, though only very rarely did I get one of these. In every letter from Granny there was the happy thought that we would meet again.

When permission was given to send two pounds of food to Holland per month, I sent whatever I could and whatever was legal to my family there and went without it myself. In her letters, Granny always rejected this help. She did not want me to deprive my growing children of any food to support old people who were "fading out." She and Aunt Betty were living on happy memories. These few letters from occupied Holland were always full of hope. They became my guiding stars during the time that more and more bombs fell around us and the war began to concentrate on the Rhineland. And so 1940 came to an end.

In peacetime there had always been a circle of good friends with us to celebrate the arrival of a new year in Gruiten. Now only one was left, the former chief of the Wuppertal obstetrical school, a well-known gynecologist my father's age. When the Hitlerites seized power, he was sacked from his important job, which he had held for eighteen years, because he was a Freemason and Rotarian—societies that, in the Nazi view, were not national but too international. Fighting for his rights, he ended in misery. The Reichsärzteführer Dr. Conti even took away his license. This fight took all his money, and his home in Barmen had been bombed three times. This beaten old man came to Gruiten to look back with us on a dreadful year. We sat around the fireplace. Everybody was lost in his own thoughts.

On the last day of 1940, Alex got his draft notice. Having been born in 1902, he had never done any military service. There this peaceful man sat before the fire. He could not grasp it. He had been called to work in the war machine.

We decided not to tell anybody about this, to avoid unnecessary questions. Most people thought that someone who worked for the food sector would not be called up. It may also have seemed strange that the husband of a "non-Aryan," which meant a "politically unreliable" person, had to do military service. None of this seemed to matter. The men born in 1902 had to join the forces. After all, there was still his wife, me, who had learned poultry farming and knew all about soup fabrication. Probably this was the reason that Alex could leave.

After he had had a few weeks of military training, I was permitted to visit him in Mühlheim on the Ruhr. He looked pale and strained when I saw him waiting for me at the platform gate. He pressed a rolled-up newspaper to the collar of his uniform. Our greetings seemed short and formal. It was cold and we walked through strange, unfriendly-looking streets. At every crossing Alex looked aside, as though for an officer he would have to salute. He was glad when this was not necessary. He was always afraid of drawing attention.

I also finally learned why he kept pressing the newspaper against his collar: it covered an empty buttonhole. At that time he did not yet know the trick of pushing a match through the loop. I went into a haberdashery shop to buy a needle and thread. They asked me for a coupon from my clothes card. I did not have it with me. After I explained my worries to the kind-looking shopkeeper, she disappeared in her apartment behind the shop and returned with a threaded needle, which she handed to me, saying, "Take it. After all, he defends us too!"

We went into a small coffee shop, where we bought two poor-looking cakes with our bread-ration coupons. Every bite swelled in our mouths, and it took me a long time to fasten the button. Meanwhile Alex told me that they would be moving out in two days. There we sat in a cheap little café. We had to look at other soldiers kissing their girls. We thought we did not belong among them. But that didn't help.

When we left, it was already dark. I had to catch a train to get the connection to Gruiten. Alex had to be back at the barracks. Slowly we walked toward the station.

Suddenly he grabbed my arm and stopped me. In a totally changed and excited voice he asked me, "Tell me, why did you insist on me making my will? I did intend to leave you all I have!"

"Well, my dear, you ask me why? I still feel that I am in danger because of my Jewish extraction. The laws on the possessions of non-Aryans could become stricter still, and if I had it all, they might take it all away from me. What would be left for our children? Let's not talk about it. I'm certain you'll be coming home again. Let's not think about it. It's morbid. Agree?"

"No, I *don't* agree. I don't understand, Tutti! You never

used to think you were in so much danger! There must be something else behind all this, something I don't know about, and that worries me no end."

"Don't worry," I said, but it was hard to say "Don't think about it anymore. All will turn out well in the end!"

At the station we separated quickly. Two days later Alex's unit moved into France. He became a clerk in a motor pool.

With the children, the staff, and my two enterprises—the poultry farm and the soup factory—I was now on my own in Gruiten.

The air raids on the Ruhr increased constantly. Not a single night passed without the sound of the sirens, and we heard the Allied squadrons fly over us. I sat at the radio to hear the news about the directions of the fighters and bombers, so I could call the children and the staff to the air raid shelter we had built in the basement. Until then only a few bombs had fallen on our area. Our work was not disturbed. It went on normally. Months passed like this.

One beautiful morning I was working in the vegetable garden along the main road, hacking rows of beans. My thoughts were with my family in Hamburg and my husband in France. I did not see one of my farmer neighbors stop near me. He had two men with him; I did not know them. They all watched me as I worked.

When I saw them at last, my neighbor started to talk: "What about it, doctor? Wouldn't you like a few of these Polish pigs for your farm? You can't manage all your work with the little help you have. You just apply for a few of these chaps and you will get some when the next transport arrives. You just pick them up. You don't need to feed them and, when they don't work, just give them a kick in the pants! I was told that this is the way to treat them, when I signed the paper, after getting these fellows. I just signed, as if they were things from the store. It would be best to let them all die. They started the war and we now get the bombs on our roofs!"

While he was talking, I stopped hacking the beans and

looked up. Mincing no words, I declared that I was not going to have any prisoners on my farm. They were human beings just like everybody else. They had to have food, clothes, shelter, and warmth in winter. I was certain that I would give all this to prisoners in my place, and probably still more. I also realized that, with such an approach, I could be blamed for coddling prisoners and therefore I would be shot. No thanks, I said. I would manage with my own staff and that was that. I continued to hack the beans.

The Polish prisoners, who were sent to do agricultural work, proved to be good workers. They were told strictly that every approach to Germans was forbidden and would be punished severely. One day a Pole was found in the hay with a German girl. Perhaps he had been denounced by a jealous rival. The man was hit heavily and brought to the police station, where he was locked up. Early the next morning, at four o'clock, I heard the strangely deadened roll of a drum on the road before the house. The sound got closer, then faded away. Standing behind the curtain of my bedroom window, I saw the village policeman with the drum. He was followed by Polish prisoners in a long gray line, which looked like a huge colorless snake. At the end was a second policeman, waving his pistol. I went to the other side of the house and saw the group disappear in the forest. Shivering, I went back to bed.

Later I heard that an old quarry had been their goal. Some of the old beeches stood close to the edge, their roots clinging to the rocks, their branches reaching out. Here the policemen stopped the Poles. A rope with a loop was thrown over a low branch, and one of the delinquent's compatriots had to pull the noose around the victim's neck. Four others, who had drawn lots, had to hold the rope, while one of the policemen pushed the offender into the quarry. All Poles who worked in Gruiten were forced to attend this gruesome scene, as a warning.

That day I went into the forest with my big Alsatian dog and my walking stick, as I always did when outside the fence. I was determined to have the tree where the hanging had occurred cut down if it stood on my estate, even without the permission of the Forestry Department. On the way I met a neighbor who probably had the same thought. Long before I could meet him, his she-hound came running to play with my Alsatian.

"The tree is on my estate, doctor," the old gentleman said. "I admit that I am too much of a coward to cut it down without permission. Let us hope that nothing similar will happen again!"

We shook hands. We knew how we felt about the present political situation, and we were friends. We went home. For a while the dogs still ran happily together across the meadows. Then, with a whistle, I called mine back to me.

The next morning I got the long-expected letter from France. Alex gave me his postal number and told me that a small parcel with some candles and a shimmy was on the way for me. Then came a heavily underlined question: "Could I perhaps give you some pleasure by sending you a corset?"

This was a real soldier's word which had stuck in the vocabulary of people who went to France, where such gadgets were important in Parisian life, to shape all the necessary bulges on female bodies, which makes France French. I was extremely amused and astonished at this request, but I soon understood: The village where Alex was stationed at this time had a corset-making center, and all his comrades had placed orders for their wives. So Alex wanted my measurements and asked if I would please send them soon, because they did not know how long they would be in that area.

Poor Alex, he was trying to give me a present from a country that had already been pillaged. He must have been very disappointed when I rejected his kind offer.

The drab daily routine went on, without any mail at all, either from Alex or from Holland or Hamburg. Time passed slowly.

Until that time every German could decide for himself whether to fly a black, white, and red flag, or the red one with the Swastika in the center. My house could be seen from far away, being in a beautiful position on the edge of the forest, but it was also easy to make it out from the railway line. One day a telephone order came from the chief of the local Party branch: "Fly a flag tomorrow." Early the next morning, my large black, white, and red flag flew from the first-floor balcony. Later a large car stopped at the garden gate and three big SA men with beautifully polished boots marched to the door. They were high-ranking Party members in the village.

"*That* flag has to come down!" one of them yelled at me.

"Well, why?" I asked. "I was told on the phone to fly a flag, and, as you see, I did!"

"I want to tell you, doctor, that the Swastika flag has to fly from this beautiful house which is visible from far away!"

"But, as far as I know, I can decide—"

"You can't decide a *thing* anymore. *You* deciding is a thing of the past! In the future *we* will be the ones to decide whether you will be able to fly a flag at all! Or you yourself soon will hang as a flag—on a gallows in a concentration camp! Anyway, you may think it over. This flag has to come down at once. Don't worry about going up there; we are going to take it with us immediately, so you won't make a mistake again. And remember that we are able to watch your house from Party headquarters, with field glasses. We always can see what flag you fly!"

I opened the door so that the three could go upstairs to take down the flag. But this was not their idea of male efficiency. One of them bent down, the second jumped on his back, and the third climbed on the shoulders of the second. From there he climbed on the balcony, took the flag off, and came down the same way. Then between them the flag was neatly folded like a bed sheet.

"Order from the Party leader, doctor: Buy yourself a new Swastika flag!"

They marched back to the car and drove off.

I knew at once what I had to do. At the grocer's I bought one of those tiny flags that children waved when foreign royalty came to visit. The next time I was told to a fly a flag, I squeezed the thin stick of the tiny flag into the ring that had held the staff of my former large flag. Probably nobody could see it from the Party office, even with field glasses.

Soon the three important functionaries were at my door again. Without saluting, one of them yelled at me, "What does this flag mean?"

"It is the Swastika flag I was ordered to fly!" I snapped.

"But not as small as that!"

"Nobody told me the size!"

"Since you are not willing to buy yourself a large Swastika flag which can be seen from far away, doctor, we shall do it for you. The sheriff will bring the correct flag C.O.D. and you will pay at once! But don't forget: You are being watched!"

They marched off. I felt sick. The Party continued to advise me on when to fly a flag.

———

One day I was sitting at my desk under the large window above the street. I saw Oskar coming home from school. He usually passed the basement, left his schoolbag in the hall, and came into my room to tell me what he had learned and about things that had happened. Today, though, Oskar did not come to me. I went into the kitchen and found my eight-year-old son there. He had his head down on the table, and his whole body was shaking with wild sobs. I asked what terrible thing had happened to him.

Wildly, with an expression of despair, he threw up his head and cried, "The Führer blind in Landsberg!" he exclaimed, still sobbing, and sank down again.

"What's the matter?" I asked. "What happened?"

"Oh, Mum, it's too terrible! Our beloved Führer in Landsberg is blind! Oh, gee, how terrible that is!" He started sobbing again.

Only slowly did I understand: Hitler's life story had been

told in school. For Oskar, Hitler's suffering seemed worse than the suffering of the Lord's Passion, which was told to the children *after* Easter.

This episode took place in the kitchen before lunch. The two maids, the farmhand, and the poultry assistant were waiting for me to serve them their meal. I had the strange feeling that one of the maids was waiting for me to make a rash remark. She would have denounced me to the Party at once, and the rest of the staff would be called as witnesses. She looked like a toad behind a stone, waiting for its prey. I pulled myself together to keep from saying anything and suddenly remembered a story Oskar had recently told me about school.

The teacher had asked a boy in the class, "Well, was your father pleased with the last speech of the Führer?"

The boy got up and naively answered, "My father turns the radio off whenever the Führer speaks!"

The teacher reported this to the Party leader. Early the next morning the child's father was taken away, being considered "politically irresponsible." He never came home.

Without saying a word, I served lunch. The children had their meals with the staff in the comfortable kitchen corner. I took my part of the food to my desk and continued to work. There was no time to waste.

Soon another "school problem" came up. It began with a question after Oskar's return. He was quite excited about something. I was seized with terror when I heard him ask, "Say, Mum, what is a Jew?"

"Jews, my son," I began hoarsely, "are human beings like you and me. But they have a different creed. They do not believe that our Lord Jesus was born at Christmas at Bethlehem. They are still waiting for their Savior."

"No, Mum, that must be different somehow," the child insisted. "In school today our teacher said that the Jews are our misery. Please, Mum, honestly, tell me; is that true?"

"I am afraid you did not understand your teacher properly, Oskar." I tried to change the subject, realizing the danger.

"But, Mum," the boy continued imperturbably, "there is the boy Kussel in my class. He sits in the same row as I do. He started to cry bitterly when the teacher said that about the Jews. So the teacher asked him why he was howling. So Kussel said that his father was a Jew and that the SS had fetched him early one morning. And when he said the word 'fetched,' poor little Kussel could not continue speaking anymore at all, he cried so! Mum, please, Mum, what did he mean by 'fetched'?"

I couldn't say anything. Because there is no way of getting around children's questions, I changed the subject: "Come, we'll go to the farm together, my boy. Today you are allowed to give me a hand. Just for today you may do your schoolwork when it gets dark. Won't that be nice?"

"Of course it is, Mum!" Oskar replied happily. And so the young Kussel was forgotten, at least for the moment.

———

It looked as though 1941 was going to bring me nothing but problems. Now the change of staff began. The nice young poultry assistant hurt himself while cutting wood with an ax. He came into the kitchen so that I could bandage his finger. When he noticed the small pool of his blood on the tiled floor, he fainted. He fell, face first on the stove. He broke his nose and had his front teeth knocked loose. I had to drive him to our hospital. Before he could begin work on the farm again, he was drafted.

Now I expanded my "soup factory." I made some alterations in the basement. Then I bought a large soup boiler. The money came from my small attic business. At the beginning of the war, I had produced a ton and a half of my product each month. At that time my whole output was confiscated for military hospitals and troop transports. I had become an army supplier in miniature. I employed a representative for the sale.

Because I was running a vital food-sector enterprise, I was

due to get a new helper for the poultry farm, but I had to agree to whatever I got. The employment bureau in Mettmann sent me a certain G., who could not do military service because of a blind eye and a short leg. G. came to present himself. I looked at his work permit, which clearly showed that he was constantly changing jobs. An appendix had already been fastened to the book, because the original pages had no room left to list all his jobs. G.'s references all showed that he had left "of his own desire." I asked how much pay he wanted. The figure fit my calculations. We settled the time-off: one afternoon every week and every second Sunday. I signed the employment-office card and hired G.

He started his new job punctually the next morning. He was wearing an SA uniform. He declared that he would be busy until lunchtime, decorating his room. He dragged a heavy suitcase into his room and hammered in nails to the rhythm of the "Horst Wessel Lied." For lunch he appeared in an old SA uniform. Afterward I showed him his duties on the poultry farm. It all went well for a few weeks. Then the maids refused to clean his room. I had a look at it. All the walls were decorated with huge Swastika flags. Pictures of all the high Nazi officials were exhibited. The space under his bed was full of empty beer bottles, bread crusts, old cartons, and newspapers. Since nothing could be pushed under it anymore, the heelmarks of his boots showed that further garbage would be stamped under the bed. It all was full now. I decided to ask G. to clean his room on the next working Sunday.

When the Sunday came, G. appeared in his best uniform, for breakfast. I informed him that it was his working Sunday. He told me that he had other duties, for the Party.

I stuck to our contract and declared, "This is your service Sunday, G.! I don't care a hoot whether you want to attend a church choir, the meeting of a bowling club, or the roll call of the SA. You stay here and work!"

"I see, doctor, you compare the Führer's SA with a bowling club. That's going too far! That's a defamation of the Führer! Who are you, after all? I've been thinking you're not where you should be—with your own race, I could also say? I shall report the happening to the Party!"

Without breakfast he marched through the gate.

The phone rang the following morning.

"Mettmann 831," I answered.

"Dr. Wenzel?" a man's voice asked.

"Yes."

"Dr. Wenzel is ordered to appear tomorrow at ten A.M. with all papers of ancestors at the district office of the NSDAP in Mettmann."

He hung up. I made a cup of strong coffee and began to pick out my papers. While I worked at my desk, I saw G. leaving my estate, dragging his big suitcase. I was glad. I found a letter of his on the kitchen table. He asked me to pay his salary into a certain account. He was unable to accept money from the hand of a "Jewess."

In Mettmann it was not the district Party office that checked my papers, but the Gestapo. The SS officer who did the job was more polite than I had expected. He also asked me to show all the papers regarding the parentage of my grandmother Burchard. I had the right document. It was the one my mother had brought me from father. I took it from my handbag and showed it to the official. "His Majesty King Friedrich Wilhelm III" made a deep impression on the SS man. He did not check the dates. He took a card from a file cabinet and wrote something on it. Then my papers were returned to me and I could leave.

When I sat in my car again, I felt uneasy. Without starting the motor, I opened the brake and rolled downhill. Somewhere in the valley the car stopped. With tear-blinded eyes I looked through the car window into the landscape and wholeheartedly thanked my father for the document. It had saved my life.

———

The general persecution of the Jews in Germany went on. They were forced to wear a square of yellow material into which a purple Star of David was woven, so that it would be visible on their clothes. Everybody would thus be able to recognize a Jew from a distance. Jews were forbidden to use public transport, so as not to annoy "Aryans" by their presence. Every small coupon of their food cards was stamped with a thick black $J = $ Jew. Every shop could refuse to handle such coupons.

Rumors told of Jewish transports to unknown destinations. Some people had seen Jews lined up in long rows, each person carrying a suitcase. There was talk of concentration camps. People whispered, talked, guessed. . . .

Then there was a call from a public phone box:

"Are you on the phone, Gertrud?" a man's voice asked.

"Yes," I answered. "Who's speaking?"

"This is Fritz. Today they have taken our granny away for slaughter."

"My God, that can't be possible!"

"Yes, she is gone. With a transport to Theresienstadt. But we know, of course, what *that* means. But I shouldn't phone this way. Your phone may be tapped. Could you help me?"

"Of course, with pleasure. What can I do for you?"

"As a non-Aryan I have to join the Organization Todt in two days. To 'dig,' as they say. We are not going to get any clothes and I only have my town clothes. Could you please give me some warm clothes from Alex: a jacket, a pair of trousers, and perhaps a pair of leggings and whatever you may think of? I would be grateful for anything. It really would be a great help!"

I found an absolutely disturbed family in Elberfeld. The grandmother was a Jewish widow. Her husband, an "Aryan," had passed away many years before. Since his death she had lived with her son and her daughter-in-law who had looked after her to perfection, and the two grandsons had spoiled her no end. Now she was gone.

"And if one day you get my urn by mail, Martha," Fritz told his wife, "then they have killed me themselves, these German pigs! I heard that some of the shed leaders themselves placed light signals on the roofs. Then they drove far away into their quarters, and, after a certain time, German bombers destroyed the sheds and everybody in them. Then the newspapers say they were killed by 'enemy bombers.' A fine death that is! I am ready for everything, and it would be wise, Martha, if you too could get used to such thoughts!"

Silently we sat together until I drove off again. I had put the big parcel with clothing down into the entrance quietly, when I arrived. How small such help seemed!

I wonder how often I said to myself that year, "I wish 1941 with all its horrors was over!" Now it was summer. One of father's mice cards arrived. How the children had been looking forward to getting it! I read the verses to them. Then Oskar and Alexa stood close to each other, excitedly admiring the happenings in the mouse family. When they had had enough, I noticed a remark on the margin that I had overlooked before: "Please don't send any more mail to the Innocentiastrasse. We are moving."

For a long time there was no letter for me, but the mice cards for the children arrived punctually. Then I had a phone call from the chief of the railway goods department in Gruiten: Would I please pick up some furniture and two pieces sewn into sacking? And this, please, the same day. He wanted to get rid of the stuff, because every air raid during the night could endanger my possessions. What could it all be about? I took the car out of the garage, hung on the trailer, and drove to the station.

Dr. E. Burchard had given a Hamburg shipper the order to send me an antique inlaid German chest-of-drawers, and an inlaid table from Lombardy, and there were two packings with Persian rugs, as I read on the bill of lading. I could not grasp it. What had happened in Hamburg to make my parents give up these things they had always lived with?

There was still no mail. Then a long-time friend of mine wrote me a letter with the facts that I had guessed: Jews were forbidden to live among "Aryans" in good sections. Old and dilapidated dwellings had been made available for the Jews. A paragraph declared that five square yards were to be assigned to each Jew. As a married couple, my parents got one tiny room and one still tinier one, which counted as a half-room. My friend had visited them. He said that mother had shown taste and skill in making their home livable. He had an old acquaintance, a widow, on the same floor and he told me that he was extremely happy that these three old ones could form a happy community. The widow was extremely grateful that mother would cook for her too. Father would serve her simple meal. Acting as an exquisite butler, he would bring her the meal on a tray, and he always had an encouraging word or a little joke ready for her.

Thus it became father's pleasure to look after his two ladies. Early riser as he was, he walked to the market, the folded-up briefcase carefully pressed against the large yellow Jewish Star on his coat. At the market he bought inexpensive fish, and occasionally a chicken, some vegetables, salads, and above all flowers. With these he made his two ladies happy. Now they could embellish their little rooms!

In the afternoon he might sit on the Elbbrücken in the sun, to smoke his cigar. (I sent him some money every month for this private pleasure.) Then he might speak a few words to his neighbor, chat with a sailor about pretty girls, or watch children playing. After such a relaxing afternoon, he walked home. Then he sat down at his little table to write. In his extremely kind, warmhearted, and humorous way, he would compose the verses for the next mice card for his Gruiten grandchildren.

While father helped his two ladies endure life in their cage, mother settled in her tiny household and knit for my children. She never left her room. She did not know how to cover up her Jewish Star, and she now had difficulty in walking. Because all public transportation was forbidden to her, she stayed at home.

Sometimes one of my good friends went to visit my parents, despite the danger of being followed and then denounced. ("Aryans" were forbidden to visit Jews.) My friends always told me how nice their little home looked. They were touched that father always poured out a tiny glass of brandy and that mother always put a single biscuit at the side of the glass. She always sat sewing or knitting near the window. One friend gave me his impressions of my parents: "I only can say that your parents live true to the laws they have set out for themselves. Father epicurean. Mother humble, cautious, working with her needle."

Their address was 1 Papagojenstrasse, Altona. In this way Ellen Burchard, née Warburg, returned to Altona, to one of the most miserable quarters near the port. In the years before her marriage she might have known the area as an active social worker, when she went there from the Palmaille. Now they were living there themselves. My friend's letter ended with this sentence: "Their surroundings did not change them."

––––––––

The winter of 1941 to 1942 was exceptionally cold. The soldiers who survived it in Russia were decorated with a special medal, which the man on the street called the "Freezing" or "Tremble" Medal. This was a cheap joke by people who had passed the winter in heated rooms and behind unbroken windows.

Alex endured this winter in Russia, where his unit had been transferred. For weeks he had been on the train from Bordeaux in France to Kharkov in the Ukraine, far behind the front. In short letters, he emphasized that there was nothing to complain about. He asked me to send him some soup cubes. These were my private provisions for the families of his comrades. I was happy to give them. In return, the soldiers' wives sent me goods from the surplus of their businesses. In this way we once got six rolls of toilet paper, an indescribable luxury!

The fuel supply for the German population during this cold winter was very poor. Some people managed to get something on the black market, but it was tremendously expensive. Others jumped from bridges onto moving coal trains and threw coal down to their children, who ran beside the train to pick it up. This was really dangerous.

Others asked me for permission to gather wood in my forest. On small pieces of paper with my signature, I allowed the holder to pick up dry branches, cut them up, and carry them home in bags. All were people who lived in the area and were known to me. The paper had to be shown to my "forest inspector" on demand. As planned, it started with picking up branches. Then stones were fastened to strong ropes, which were thrown over thick branches and pulled down. In the end the beeches were cut down, sawed into large logs, and carried home. The remnants of the trees seemed to groan as they were taken past my house. I looked the other way. The people were freezing.

As for us, we heated the kitchen with its stove and the lounge with an iron stove, installed when the central heating was cut off for lack of coal. In the evening, when the kitchen stove was out, six of us sat together in my room.

One member of the group was the old farmhand Büscher, a former miner, who had once been buried in a cave-in and now lived on a pension. He was a wise and quiet man. During sixty years of life he could not remember seeing the sun for twenty, as he told me. Before the sun rose, he went into the mine, and the sun had already set when he went home. He worked extra shifts on Sundays and holidays, because he had a large family. For many years, he said, he saw his children only when they were asleep.

Then there was the poultry farm assistant, Alfred, who had followed the SA man, G. Alfred was too small for military service. He was only five feet tall, and looked very square, but he was rather strong. His huge head sat squarely on his shoulders. His legs were short, so that he could not reach the floor when he sat on a chair. His legs would dangle restlessly all evening. As he sat, he would join his hands on his knees and turn his thumbs in different ways, which he said was very hard to do.

Then there was my long-time maid, Paula, who was embroidering a tablecloth for her dowry. Last but not least came the three Wenzels. At that period the employment office did not allow me any household apprentices anymore. Because I was considered a "politically unreliable" person, the Party had taken away my teaching diploma.

Büscher smoked his own tobacco. Tobacco had long been

rationed and could be obtained only with certain coupons. In the country every man was allowed to plant up to fifty-nine tobacco plants for himself. A tax had to be paid as soon as he had sixty plants, and most then had to be delivered to an official collecting hall. So Büscher and Oskar had a plantation of their own. They harvested the leaves and hung them nicely and well separated in corners of the attic. Alfred was not in on this. He did not smoke, and called the whole sport idiotic, but actually he was too lazy for it all.

At that time there were special recipes for people who wanted to ferment their tobacco leaves. These recipes were like the ones that women used to give cakes some taste with hardly any ingredients. The tobacco could be treated with sugar, rose petals, plum juice, or many other things. But then one day something horrid happened: Oskar dipped some of his tobacco leaves in a solution that contained the weekly sugar ration for six people! Not very funny for me!

One evening Oskar and I were home alone. Büscher had gone to Essen to visit his son. Paula had taken Alexa with her for church choir practice, and Alfred had already gone to bed. We sat in the dark and looked at the small flickering light on the floor, which came from the oven door. It was January and very cold.

As the only parent at home, I had long wished for a heart-to-heart talk with my son to clarify his mixed-up ideas about human reproduction. I was certain that the books Oskar had read and his agricultural observations had muddled some things that I had to sort out. He was nine, and I thought the time had come for such a conversation.

I remembered my own youthful confused ideas. Early in my life I was told that a mother carried her child under her heart, but the thought of how it got there occupied me greatly. I was certain that it had something to do with a chemical tablet, but how did that get there? I thought, it could only be with a thermometer.

If somebody had asked me when I was my son's age what I was going to learn as a profession, I would have answered "chemist." I thought this was a good businesss for making tablets that could start a new human being. These tablets would always be in demand, because there would always be new babies in this world!

To avoid such fantasies with my son, I simply asked him what he knew about "the birds and bees."

"ALL!" he bellowed, and with this the subject seemed to be finished for him. I could not get him to pay any further attention to my project.

So it was a welcome event when the she-goat Liese had to go to the he-goat. There was much snow and it was bitterly cold. We tied an old red quilt on the animal so that she would not catch cold. I stuffed Oskar into his heaviest coat, with hood, thick gloves, and Wellingtons. Then I put Liese's halter in his hand and told him to take her over the hill to the miller's place, where the village he-goat was kept.

"And here are five Marks, which you will give to the miller, please!" I told him.

"What are the five Marks for, Mum?"

"You'll see!"

Oskar disappeared over the hill, tugging the red-covered Liese behind him, working his way through the deep snow. After some time he returned, whistling happily.

"Well?" I asked, waiting for his observations.

"Mum, is that all? I've known that a long time! What a long beard he has! And how awful he stinks!"

By coincidence I was not home when Liese gave birth to twins. Oskar delivered them. He thought it all quite normal, as he told me.

———

Every day I wrote a letter to Alex, and the postman who came in the morning took it with him. At the beginning of the war I had started to note down the news of the day in a kind of diary made of typing paper. After about two weeks this report was finished and sent to Alex and my friends. I could not get anything but green paper in those days, so these reports were called "The Green Leaves." Some of the dates mentioned in this book have been taken from these papers.

On May 30, 1942, Alexa came into my room and called to me very excitedly: "Mum, there is a Frenchman at the kitchen door. He wants something. We can't understand him. Come out there, will you?" I went.

"*Bon jour, Madame. Parlez-vous français?*" he asked me, bowing politely. He was a French prisoner of war. His uniform was neat and clean.

"*Oui, qu'est ce que vous désirez, Monsieur?*"

"*Rien pour moi, Madame, mais notre cuisinier voudrait des poules.*"

I explained to the Frenchman that I could not give him any chickens. They had all been accounted for officially and the number would be checked. I had to hand in the legs of every hen that died on my farm and it was then deducted from the stock. With the best will in the world, I could not give him any birds. The Frenchman explained that his cook did not want to *keep* the birds. He wanted them so that he could have something alive to run around the rails of the Vohwinkel shunting station, where they had their POW camp. He did not want the eggs either. He wanted to liven up the drab view from his window; that was all. I would still own the chickens, and I could have the eggs as well!

A likely story, I thought. How could I get out of it? In the end I found a way out. We had a few ducks which did not come under the general rule. I handed four ducks to the Frenchman as a loan for his cook. They would not give any difficulties and might liven up their camp. The Frenchman bowed again, introduced himself as Louis B., and emphasized how glad he was to have made my acquaintance. In exchange, he promised to bring a bucket of kitchen garbage twice a week, for our pig. I accepted with pleasure. Then I asked him, in French, not to shake hands with me. The servants could hear us talk, but could not understand a word. They would be suspicious, however, if they saw me shaking hands with an enemy.

From that day on, Louis brought a bucket full of very thin potato peels every Tuesday and Friday.

Soon after he had gone, I received a wire by phone. Alex told me that he would be coming on leave the day after next. He would inform me of the exact train by telegram.

On June 2, 1942, we awaited our soldier. We were full of anticipation, and made many preparations for his reception. But the eagerly awaited day turned out sadly. Everything was different from what we had hoped for. A serious, deeply disturbed man came home. He had not known the harshness and cruelty of which human beings are capable. Now he had witnessed them in the war, and this had scarred him. He walked through the farm and the factory slowly and alone, after having shushed the three of us with a movement of his hand. When he returned to the house for a short time, he put his hand on my shoulder and said, "Thank you."

In the evening we sat on the terrace in the dark. Alex stared toward the forest without speaking. A bat flitted past. Alex jumped up and looked after it.

"We also have some in Russia, but they are much smaller!" a harsh voice said. Then it was silent again. And then, slowly, in a low voice, I began to tell Alex of the children, the farm, and the soup factory. With this I found a tiny hole through which I could get close to his heart. There seemed to be so little space there for the children and me. The many deaths he had seen in the war had shaken him. He had seen death only once before in his life, in the quiet face of his father, who died before we met. The suffering of the wounded and the dying must have tormented him. He may also have been haunted by the fear of the Russian civilians he encountered along the way. He did not know their language. The old ones made the sign of the cross when Germans walked past, and even when vehicles from his unit drove by. These apocalyptic images had overwhelmed him the eighteen months we had been separated. They had followed him home and he could not shake them off.

"Is that really our Daddy?" Oskar asked. This shocked me. "We are all so nice to him and he doesn't tell us anything!" the child complained.

I tried to console the boy: "Daddy has been away for such a long time. He has to get used to Gruiten again. I'm certain that everything will work out better during the next leave!"

Alex stayed for five days. He planned to visit his mother near Frankfurt, then to return to Gruiten. The night before his departure, we were silently following a moonbeam as it wandered across the beautiful grain in the inlaid wardrobe. Suddenly, all the horrors of Alex's war experiences broke out of him. He began to speak. The only way I could help him was by holding his hand. His hand was just as cold as mine.

Alex swore he had never killed a man. So far he had not been forced to defend himself, and he had not been ordered to shoot Russians or Jews. But many of the rumors we had heard were true. From participants Alex knew, he had heard of torments and cruelties, of shooting and common graves—horrors that no force on earth could make him talk about. Then, with great pain, this kind man, who had grown up in a minister's home, declared "The Lord—if there is one—is neither good nor kind!"

I did not speak a single word that night. I did not know what to say to give him help, comfort, consolation. I knew that my own people belonged to those Alex was speaking of. I also knew that *I* belonged to them.

With all that was told that night, a writer could fill volumes of horror. One of the happenings stuck in my memory:

One afternoon, on a rest day, Alex lay in the sun under a light roof of beech leaves, close to the rim of a sand pit. The forest reminded him of Gruiten. He was dreaming of home.

The harsh voice of a man giving commands pulled him out of his peaceful thoughts. Carefully, without making any noise himself, he crawled toward the edge of the pit so that he could look down into it.

Below him he saw a figure in a black SS uniform. The SS man was pointing his pistol toward a young and beautiful Jewish woman and her little daughter, who may have been four years old.

He ordered them to undress and stand with their backs to the sand wall. They were going to die, he said.

The little girl turned toward her mother, looked up to her, and asked, "Mum, does it hurt to die?"

Two shots cracked loudly. . . .

After witnessing all this Alex no longer felt "pure," he told me. He said it was impossible to remain the person he had been before he had left. Everything was fading away in the hell of the war: his parents' home, the teaching of his minister father. His early childhood prayers were just sliding away, and so was his belief in God. The thought of human kindness had been burned out, as though with acid. He knew how he had changed, but he was unable to do anything about it. And it was just this knowledge that made it so terrible! There was just nothing left to hold on to, nothing at all. He did not belong to Gruiten anymore, or to his home town, where he was to visit his old mother the next day. What was he going to tell her? He knew that the old woman believed in God and he was certain that she would be praying for him every night. He was afraid of destroying something if he spoke out honestly. He shuddered as he thought of that visit.

After telling me all this, Alex felt better, he said, and he thanked me for my patience. All the talk, and the excitement of recalling all the events of the war in Russia, had tired him out. He fell asleep and slept for a long time. Early the next morning I crept out of the room to attend to my work.

During his leave I had not been Alex's wife.

Soon after he left to see his mother, a wire came from his unit: Military driver Alexander Wenzel had to end his leave and return to his post at once. Alex returned to the Eastern Front directly from Frankfurt. The encirclement of Stalingrad had begun.

———

Although food was strictly controlled and parcels checked, some gifts could still be sent. Father's old secretary had agreed that I should send her his birthday parcel. She would then hand it to him in the crowd at the fish market.

On June 30, 1942, I sent father a small wooden box with a duck, already slightly roasted, a jar with black currant jelly, which he especially liked, and a bottle of good red Burgundy wine, which he had preferred during his last stay in Gruiten.

Everything worked out perfectly. Even before mother could finish roasting the duck, father wrote me one of his touching letters. He told me that the parcel had arrived punctually on July 6 and that it was a real birthday treat!

On the evening of July 9 I got a call from a trunk exchange public phone in Hamburg. Mother's sister Ada was on the phone. She seemed completely distraught. From what she said I gathered that my parents, as Jews, had gotten their expulsion order and would be evacuated to the East on July 11. Mother had left their small apartment to visit a neighbor. While she was out, my father had taken an overdose of sleeping pills. When mother returned, she found him unconscious on his bed. She informed the police. They brought father—at his own expense, it was emphasized—to the Jewish hospital, Johnsallee, in Hamburg. Mother got permission to accompany him and stayed at his side. Aunt Ada reported that father's stomach had been pumped out but that he could not be brought out of his coma. He was still alive—if one can call it that—when mother was picked up in a police car and transported back to the Papagojenstrasse in Altona. The order said that she had to leave there on the morning of July 11.

"Are you still there, Gertrud?" my aunt asked.

"Yes. I am coming to Hamburg at once!"

"Listen, my dear," my aunt said, "your mother strictly asks you *not* to come! You can't help anybody and you would only put your children and yourself in danger if you come to Hamburg! Do you hear me, mother asks you *not* to come! She is quite definite!"

The operator interrupted: "The three minutes Hamburg has paid for are expired. I need the line for other purposes. I have to cut you off."

A few days later, I got an open postcard from my mother, dated July 11, 1942. She had written it while sitting on her suitcase on the platform before her train left. Mother told me how well equipped she was for a winter in the East, with warm clothes and a sleeping bag. She had also taken some knitting needles with her; she thought she might be able to earn some money by knitting. And she wrote that she would always think of us and that she was certain that all would be well.

One day after this card, another one arrived, the last mice card from my father to his grandchildren:

This is the end of the mouse story:

> *Happily home moves the family of mice.*
> *The picture is not new but nice.*
> *You see on it much wurst and cheese.*
> *Family Wenzel goes out on a stroll*
> *led by a tail rosy and droll.*
> *Missing alone is Father Mouse*
> *eagerly awaited in his house.*
> *Once the whole family is there*
> *Sun and happiness will rise like a flare!*

Across this happy tale my father, who had long planned his suicide, had written:

> *Der Mäuseahne sinkt ins **Grab***
> *Und blickt auf die Enkel segnend herab.*
>
> *The mouse grandfather sinks into his grave*
> *And with blessings looks down on his grandchildren.*

Father had always said, "They won't get *me!* When life is not worth living anymore, I'll finish it myself."

Mother, though, had always told herself, "Father is not going to do himself any harm. Dogs who bark don't bite! I don't believe that old people like me will be murdered. I intend to empty my goblet to the dregs, because I want to see my children again!"

The name of the goblet was: AUSCHWITZ.

Who could have told Granny about the removal of her daughter and the death of her son-in-law? I expect that Aunt Ada, her second daughter, had to take on this heavy task. She had been married to an "Aryan" and, though now widowed, was classified as "Christian-Jewess." As such she was not really in danger in 1942, when all this happened. So she witnessed the end of her sister and her brother-in-law in Hamburg.

We got less and less news from Holland. I heard that Granny was very weak and could hardly see anymore. Letters from Germany and flowers, which members of the Église Wallonne brought her, were her greatest pleasure.

Neither Granny nor Aunt Betty ever mentioned anything about the death of my parents.

The air raids on the Rhineland became worse. A new word appeared in army news reports—a word that became a fixation: terror attack. The news on the radio gave us not only the flight direction for an air raid by Allied planes, but also the number of planes. Most of the air raids came at night. Between the details given, a metronome hacked time into pieces. . . .

From our house, which was situated on higher ground near the forest, we could see the gleaming flares marking the squares where the bombs would be dropped: Düsseldorf, Cologne, Duisburg, Essen, Wuppertal, Solingen. We knew what that meant. We could imagine how these cities would look after a terror attack. The people had a name for the flares, which came down slowly on tiny parachutes; they called them "Christmas trees."

One morning a single bomb fell between the railway line and our house. Probably it was released to destroy the railway tracks, which may have glistened in the sun. The railway remained undamaged, but the city watermain was destroyed. That was in 1943. We went without running water in the house until 1946. Meanwhile we had to get all water from a creek between the poultry farm and the forest. We used buckets, which we pulled up in a handcart. We needed a lot of water for the household, the farm, and the factory. In those years I learned to be careful with water. The dishes were washed with potato-cooking water. With this washing-up water the tiled kitchen floor was cleaned, and then the water was collected in a bucket to be poured down the WC. We got used to all this.

In June 1942 Alex returned to Kharkov. He wrote only rarely. In his letters he emphasized that he was well and that I should not worry. As a special Christmas treat, I had the children talk on a phonograph record. I mailed it early and hoped it would arrive on time. Oskar liked the idea of telling his father some stories. He began by saying that we had slaughtered a pig. It would be a full meat ration for five people for a year. When the meat inspector came, everything but the tongue and a good roast was already in tins. The official took both pieces with him, the child said. Then Oskar sang a few Christmas carols for his father, happily mingling them with other popular songs.

Alexa accompanied her brother's efforts with tiny little crying noises in the background. We could not get her to record any words.

I got a tiny scribbled note from Alex. It was dated "Beginning of November 1942." He said he had been ordered to join a special unit and would be sent to the front immediately. I should not expect any mail from there. If something happened to him, and he was not able to write to me again, he wanted to thank me for everything I had done for him. He wished us all a happy Christmas.

Then there was no news anymore. I continued writing every evening and addressed the letters to field-post number 38133. I waited for weeks, months, several months. No letters came from the East. I wrote to Alex's commanding officer, whose name I knew, and to the wives of some of his comrades, whose addresses I knew from sending them some of my soup cubes. I asked if they knew anything of Alex's fate. I got polite, restrained answers. It was stressed again and again that it was forbidden to give any information about comrades. All letters contained this sentence. It was unbearable.

Somebody, who may have had some pity on me, gave me the private address of their commander in the Palatinate. I wrote a letter to this address, but did not get any answer.

A lonely Christmas passed, without any news. On New Year's Eve my old medical friend and I were alone. We had lighted the fire as a festive luxury. We sat in the dark, watching the flames. The windows were dark. It was very, very quiet.

"Gertrud," the trusted friend said, "I am as old as your father. Tonight I would like to replace him. I can't stand seeing how you're ruining yourself waiting for mail. You have to think about your children. Believe me, I mean well: Please get used to the idea that your husband may have been killed in the war. If this isn't true, so much the better. Then the happiness will blot out this conversation. With all my heart I hope Alex will return, but I don't believe it anymore."

There was no further mail from the East. At the beginning of March 1943 I got a postcard from the station at Vohwinkel. It had the printed words "Will you kindly pick up," and then a handwritten addition: "one box of goods owned by a fallen soldier."

That was the first news. I could not believe it. I thought there was an error in the address. Out of my mind, I took the car out of the garage and drove to Vohwinkel. I presented my card at the goods department. The official was totally indifferent, since he already had done so many of his jobs that day. He walked around his hall, comparing numbers and boxes. Then he took a book from his high desk, opened it, made a little cross near "Wenzel," and showed me where to sign on the line beside the name. I did it all absolutely automatically and got the box. I lifted it.

"There are still five cents to pay for the postage of the card, miss!" the official called. I paid without saying anything.

Then I picked up the box and carried it to the car. It was a French champagne carton. The brand was painted on in big letters. A few champagne glasses were also painted on. The box had a special spring lock through which wires were pulled.

I drove home and put the box in the basement. For days I

could not open it. When I finally decided to unpack it, there were books, clothes, and the unopened box with the children's record, Alex's Christmas gift. There were no personal belongings in the box—no wallet, no watch, no old letters or photographs, nothing of that kind.

When Alex left, he had given me his wedding ring and said, "For your widow's ring!"

I thought this remark unnecessary and cruel. His ring was in the safe. There it lay. I still had no official news. My heart still hung on the thin but strong thread called *HOPE*.

In mid-March I got a short letter from Aunt Betty. She said that Granny was not well. Because of the little food they had and the cold in their flat all winter, the old woman seemed to fade away. Aunt Betty was not well either, but the most important thing was to help the old lady. Granny was determined to do everything she could to get better. She hoped to see us again. The kindness and help of their Dutch friends were touching, and my food parcels also helped.

Granny had added a few lines to this letter. The waviness in her beautiful handwriting showed clearly how shaky she was, and it was easy to tell how poor her eyesight had become. But her writing was again full of confidence and the anticipation of inviting my children and me for a holiday with her on the Dutch seaside. She had added a small picture to the letter, showing a blue hyacinth which had bloomed on her windowsill. She had painted the picture with a bird's feather, which she had picked up in the street. She had used blue ink, which she had thinned with water. Under the little picture she wrote, "Stick to nature, which will never disappoint you!"

A week later I got a long letter from Aunt Betty: They had been forced to leave their two little rooms. They had taken a small suitcase and had been put up in a "hospital." They were living with five other Jews in the same room. On the third day of their stay there, she assisted in the birth of a child, and Granny, then eighty-six and the eldest in the house, enjoyed the baby. But Aunt Betty was sorry to report that Granny was in bed, devotedly looked after by a young surgeon who was confined with them. They still had hope, to keep the flickering little flame of life burning.

The next letter with a Dutch stamp was addressed in a handwriting unknown to me. I guessed what it might contain. Madame de Bruyn, a member of the Église Wallonne, told me that my family had been deported from the Westerbork camp—which Aunt Betty had called a "hospital"—to an unknown destination in the East.

The destination's name: SOBIBOR (see Appendix).

During the war it became the custom for the head of the local N.S. Party to be informed by the unit of the death of a soldier. Then the Party official dressed himself in his best uniform, put on a crape arm band, and visited the family before they got an official letter, to bring them the sad news personally. It was said that the official's words would be a kind of congratulation that the dead man had had the honor of falling for Führer and country.

The idea of such a visit haunted me. I knew myself well enough to know that I would lose my self-control in such a meeting. I was saved from it. The official did not come to see me.

At the end of June 1943 I got the official information. The commander of Alex's unit told me, in the official set way, that the driver Alexander Wenzel had fallen for Führer and country on November 30, 1942, on the Eastern Front, during his military duty.

Like every other German soldier's widow I went to the city hall, for me Gruiten. I handed in the notice and received a stamped document concerning Alex's death. At the same time I was given an envelope with forty extra clothes coupons, for mourning garments.

The first days after I got the final news, I could not tell the children anything. There was so much business to attend to that I had no time to think. But when I began to wear the clothes that had been dyed black, the children looked surprised at this change. I told them that their father had fallen.

"I think your black stockings are hideous! And that mourning crape, or whatever that thing on the middle of your arm is called, looks like a flag at half-mast!"

Oskar made these remarks at the age of not quite ten years. Alexa was two years younger:

"I really don't understand it all, Mum. Did Dad get hurt, or is he dead?"

I told my children that their Dad was dead.

His children then cried bitterly.

Weeks later I got a letter from the commanding officer, written during his leave. He sent me a detailed description of the military action in which Alex fell. The letter was dated June 30, 1943:

Dear Dr. Wenzel:

I am very sorry about the long delay of this reply to you. I know how eagerly you were looking forward to this letter. Please forgive me for the delay and do not assume that neglect was the cause of it. Circumstances beyond our control were responsible. I wish to give you a brief account of the facts.

At the start of our correspondence, I just happened to be on a short furlough. Your letter of May 29 still reached me at home. On the following day I suddenly received a cable calling me to Munich. There I had to take charge at once of a massive troop transport to the distant Southeast (front). The return trip entailed a command visit in Italy; therefore I came back only last Sunday from a journey of almost four weeks' duration. During the arduous transport operation I was unable to write or to take care of anything else.

When I started another furlough from Munich day before yesterday your last letter was handed to me.

In the meantime I often thought of you, and today I want to give you the long-delayed report.

Dear Dr. Wenzel, please believe that this is no easy task

for me. It is very, very hard for me as the Company
Commander having to fulfill my last duty toward the families
of comrades who are no longer with us.

I came to know your husband at Unit 38133. In November, 1942, he was transferred to my group. I came to
appreciate him as a good, dutiful soldier on whom I could
always rely. He was one of our best comrades. As commander I was proud of my company, which was the best
among the battalion. This was especially evident during the
battle at the Tschier. I could rely on each of my pals. At the
end of November, 1942, we were embroiled in heavy
defensive fighting at Luwmikina. On November 29 my company received orders to defend the village of Ostrowskoje
against the Russians. The big assault of the Russians took
place on November 30 around 7:00 A.M. I myself was about
one kilometer ahead with a small part of the company, north
of Ostrowskoje, directly at the Tschier. The rest of the
company, including your husband, were still back at Ostrowskoje. The Russians now attacked with massive force, trying
to penetrate the village from the East. My brave men succeeded in halting the assault. However, we suffered heavy
casualties in the course of that morning. Our battalion lost
all its officers with the exception of Captain B. and myself.
Your husband was killed by a head shot during the defensive
battle in the early morning hours of Nov 30. He was instantly
dead. May you, dear Dr. Wenzel, take comfort from the fact
that he was spared the fate of a "severely injured" falling
into the hands of the Russians. I would like to inform you
confidentially that in two instances we've had to abandon
our severely injured. And at the withdrawal from the defensive battle we were unable to take care of our beloved dead;
we were forced to leave them on the battlefield. Thus I am
unable to inform you about the grave or the last resting place
of your dear husband.

The officer added words of condolence and assured me of his
readiness to answer any further questions. There were none.

10

Alone

The houses of Gruiten cluster around the little village church like chickens around a hen. The church has such a low steeple that it hardly rose over the roofs of the houses. It is the church of the Reformed Evangelical congregation and very plain. Even the beautiful old wood carvings, representing vines and grapes, are overpainted in plain white. The cool colorless brightness makes any diversion impossible.

I was sure that the news of Alex's death had circulated in the community. I wanted to avoid meeting anyone, so I went to church late. I entered only when the last verse of the first hymn was finished. The clergyman was just stepping up to the pulpit. I carefully avoided making any noise. I walked to the last row of benches and, standing, as is the custom, said my prayer.

As soon as I sat down, all other members of the congregation who had shared the bench with me before, got up, passed me, and sat down again in another row.

This happened in the house of the Lord. Whispering, they looked around toward me and shrugged their shoulders. This happened in the eye of the Lord. The "mongrel" stayed as pariah alone on her bench. The singing of a hymn rose over it all.

Everything that was left in me from my childhood's God died that morning in the small Gruiten church.

When I got home, Oskar was excitedly running towards me: "Mum, Mum, now you will be able to bake a really fat cake! I collected coupons worth five pounds of butter, from all over the farm! Planes must have dropped them during the night! Really, they were five pounds in all. I counted them twice. Come quickly. I shall spread them all out on your desk, then you can count them again!"

Oskar was right. Allied Mosquito planes, which flew during the night over the Rhineland, did throw food coupons down. These, if used to buy food, would undermine the German economy.

When I held a match to the coupons before the eyes of my staff, Oskar was crying. His dream of a fat cake flew in tiny black pieces of ashes toward the clouds. Then I explained to my son that these were faked food coupons and that we would be taken to prison and punished hard if we redeemed loose coupons. He just could not grasp it. He had collected too hard for a butter cake and was not getting it!

About the same time clothes coupons were dropped over the Rhineland. These bore the imprint "Freie und Hansastadt Hamburg." The shops were advised to denounce immediately any buyers who tried to buy clothes with these cards; they could be arrested. A spelling error had slipped into the cards printed by the Allies. The correct term was "Freie und Hansestadt Hamburg."

The various farms in Gruiten got their food once a week by delivery van from a Vohwinkel shop.

One day I was standing on the front lawn with a client who intended to buy a young Alsatian dog. The whole litter was there. Just then the delivery van pulled up. The dog lover could not decide which animal to take. After having disposed of his box of food in the kitchen, the delivery man joined us on the lawn on his way back to his car. He was on leave from the front and was in uniform.

"I didn't know that you were also breeding Alsatians, doctor," he began. "Are they for training?"

"The buyer can decide about that," I answered. "There are some who get them trained for the police and then sell them again. Others train them for their personal safety, and still others just keep them for their pleasure. When the young dogs are out of my fence, I have nothing to do with them anymore."

"I didn't mean it like *that*, doctor! I thought you might train them for Jews, so that they will learn to bite! Oh, you don't seem to know the wonderful story. I can see it from your face. I think it tremendously funny. I recently read it in the *Stürmer:* a Jew did bite a German Alsatian!"

The dog buyer laughed heartily. I was benumbed.

"And I also want to say, doctor, that I had good luck at Barmen after the last terror attack. Just gruesome, the way that place looks! If I could get hold of a Jew, I would pull my bayonet and would just push it into him. And then it would be a special pleasure to me to turn it around a few times!"

"That would be real fun for me too!" the dog buyer added. "And how!"

"Excuse me, please, the phone's ringing!" I said and ran across the lawn toward the house. The phone had not rung at all. After a while I returned to the two men, who were eagerly talking together. "Gentlemen, I just had a call from the leader of the Alsatian Club. He said that all young dogs are confiscated for military use. These here, which you are interested in, fall under the new regulation. I'm sorry, I can't sell you any."

"What a pity!" the prospective buyer said. He left in intense conversation with the food dealer. They headed for Vohwinkel.

I did not hoard anything at the beginning of the war. But I had "organized" a few things, as it was so nicely called. There were two big stacks of roofing tiles in the courtyard, so that I could repair the roof in case of heavy bombardments. Then there were two cases with eighty square yards of windowpanes for the house and the fowl sheds, to repair them all when pieces would "break out." And near the glass was a barrel with putty. These were all goods that were not under control when the war broke out and that one was permitted to own.

Without any notification, and very surprisingly, a few weeks after the dog happening, my solicitor friend from Hamburg stood in the door, which I had opened myself. He seemed very excited and hardly greeted me. After I had closed the lounge door behind me, he asked me gruffly, "Say, Tutti, are you totally mad to write such reports and then post them with a correct return address? As if you were not endangered enough with your faked papers! I know that I am one of your very old friends and I hope you know an old proverb: 'Who courts danger will perish!' If you continue in this way *we* can't get you out if something happens. And now come on, my dear, we'll go together to the furnace and burn at once everything—everything, you understand—that could imperil you! Before all these dangerous reports get out. I'm certain, since I know you pretty well, that you still have a few copies, and they probably lie somewhere in neat order. All family letters will also be burned—all, really *all!* If they search your house, it would be the end of you! I'm certain that that's not far off, you fool!"

The old friend knew the house. He got a wash bucket from the attic and searched my room expertly. How I would have loved to have kept my mother's last postcard, written before her deportation! I held it and he pulled the bits from my hand. It was all burned. I only wished I had buried all the papers I would have loved to keep. I began to do so from then on.

But nothing kept the danger from me, as a war widow and "three-quarter Jewess." The danger approached closer and closer.

And, one day, it stood before me in person.

A central food-distribution office had confiscated the whole production of my small soup industry to be used for troop transports, at the station, for hospital trains, and for work camps of the Reichsarbeitsdienst and the Organization Todt. These units did not send their orders to the producer himself, but wanted to be visited by a representative who collected the orders. To sell my product to the official customers, I needed a representative. In 1938 an acquaintance had recommended a certain K., a middle-aged man. We heard that his financial setup was not the best, that he had to look after his family, that his manners were all right, that he would look pleasant, and that he was a professional sales representative. He would probably be willing to take the soup product as an addition to his other goods.

When K. presented himself to Alex, he asked for a payment in advance, to get new clothes, and for a car, so as to be able to see his customers. It all was within human and financial possibilities, and so Alex and K. signed a contract in which the representative got a fixed amount per month and an additional percentage of the sales. The car had to be brought to Gruiten on Friday night and should be picked up again on Monday morning.

As long as Alex was alive, all went according to the contract. As soon as K. found out that I was a widow, his approach changed instantly. He neglected his work, kept the car over the weekends, and used it for private trips. On the weekend after I had obtained Alex's death certificate, while I settled his accounts, K. asked for more money. When I refused, he went to the limit at once.

"Listen, doctor, you can't deal with me like that!" he yelled. "Now it is *my* turn! As the wife of a soldier you still had a certain protection; that's at an end now for a Jewish widow! I know very well who you are! You'd better give me the money I want!"

I refused.

"All right," K. said. "That's the way you want it."

He took out his wallet and pulled out a paper.

"This," he continued, "is the photocopy from the Hamburg registry. Both your parents are entered as Jews. And if you have two Jewish parents, *you* are a Jewess as well! I make you a proposition: If you become my lover, I'll forget all about it. No answer? All right, I shall denounce you at once for faking documents, since you stated that you are half-Jewess. And I'll also see to it that you come out of a gas oven as a tiny bit of smoke, just the same as all your family!"

So there it was. Now what I had expected for years had happened. Somebody had found out that I had not correctly filled out my papers in the way the Nürnberg Laws demanded. Now it was as far as that. I looked at K. I probably threw my head back a moment, as I used to do in great excitement. It might have looked like a gesture of pride. My silence and this little movement of my head enraged the fellow completely. He lifted his hand and roared, "Well, will you answer?!"

He did not hit me. Nobody ever has. Absolutely sure of his victory, he threw himself into an easy chair, spread his legs wide, and bent forward, his hands on his knees. He asked, "Well, when are we going to start?"

I got up from my desk and quietly asked K. for twenty-four hours to think it over. He would get his answer tomorrow.

"All right," he said. "Tomorrow I'll be back at two P.M. Meanwhile you can pack some clothes. I'll take you and the car with me. We'll go on a trip."

In silence I opened the door of my room and then the house door. I followed K. with my eyes. He left my estate with a certain pride and a rolling gait. Slowly, certain of his victory, he passed the barn, going toward the tram. After he left my sight, I closed the door. I could not think anymore.

Evening came. I had put the children to bed, gone through the farm and checked the factory, and locked the house. Now I sat in an easy chair and looked at the forest. A little owl called from far off. It was still too early for Allied air raids. Cold and absolute numbness gripped me. What would become of my children if K. managed to get me killed? As widow and "Jewess" I had fallen into the hands of a potential murderer, who was covered by the Nazi laws. The fact was immovable and clear.

Looking into the dark I remembered that my Hamburg solicitor friend had told me of a case from his practice. He had emphasized what could happen to people like me. It was the case of one of his Jewish clients, a very beautiful young woman, whose husband had already been sent to a concentration camp. An SS man had approached her, saying that she would not have to share her husband's fate, if she was willing to share his leave with him on one of the North Sea islands.

Fearing for her life, the woman had told the story to my friend and asked for his advice. He had asked her, "Do you really want to prolong your life just for the nasty length of an SS vacation? When he is sick of you, he will send you to the death chambers anyway, or do you think that he will run the risk of being brought before the judge for RASSENSCHANDE (race defilement) when one of his comrades finds out?"

I do not know the outcome of this atrocity. I can imagine. My friend ended his report: "You know, Tutti, by God, I could not kill a chicken! But I would gladly cut this guy's throat!"

This was the story I remembered as I sat at the window in the dark. I got up and walked through the house, as though saying farewell. I sat on the children's beds and caressed my children as they slept. I walked out of the house, stood on the lawn, and looked into a clear sky full of stars. Where was this Lord who would grant justice?

I thought of my old laundress in her small house on the other side of the railroad tracks. There I had a tiny suitcase with the most necessary things, also money and jewelry. It stood there in case I had to get away suddenly. I also thought of the old policeman in the Gruiten city hall. He had once told me, full of pity, that he would send his son, who was an apprentice at the baker's, with some black bread, if an arrest warrant came to the police station: a sign for me to disappear.

But something in myself told me that it was not yet as bad as that. This thought made me feel cool, superior, down-to-earth. Suddenly the tears dried up; the despair vanished. Cool thinking started. I felt I was the daughter of my solicitor father and I began to search for a way out. And I found it.

The following morning I called the police in Gruiten and asked the sergeant to be at my place at one P.M., because I was in danger. As a war widow I could ask for help. Then I called my neighbor to come to help me at one, also. Both men arrived punctually and I explained the situation. They sat smoking in my room, where they could see the street up to the barn. I said that my representative had threatened me with extortion. I was asking for their protection, because I expected the man to be there at two. They were prepared to help.

We saw K. come down the road, right on time. He wore his sergeant's uniform and as a soldier could not be touched by civilians. He passed the garden gate, swinging his arms and looking very confident. He rang the bell. I opened the door. When K. saw the policeman standing behind me, he drew his bayonet, intending to stab me. Silently the two men twisted the weapon from him. K. was very pale and his fists trembled. His excitement made me calm.

I turned toward my two protectors and asked them to wait in the hall outside my room for four minutes and then come in. But if I called for help, they should enter at once. I had to talk with K. alone for a moment.

K. and I went in. He sat down in an easy chair without being asked to do so. I kept standing. Absolutely certain of his victory, he asked, with scorn in his voice, "Well, when do we leave for our car trip?"

"Never!" I answered quietly and continued: "Yesterday you showed me your true face. Now I know what you've been planning. Because of what you found out in the Hamburg registry, you want me as your lover. And that means that you, in full knowledge of this fact, intend to commit *Rassenschande*. You intend to blackmail me for faking a document. Okay, I would like to remind you, that, in November 1938, when Jews were persecuted and Jewish belongings destroyed, my husband asked you to bring me to safety and you drove me to a hotel in Rhöndorf on the Rhine. I am certain that the police registry of hotel guests during that year still exists. That night we had adjoining rooms. If you blackmail me for faking a document, I shall commit perjury and swear that you raped me that night. And if I compare these two offenses with the eye of the

National Socialist ideal and the Nürnberg Laws, falsification of a document to Rassenschande, I am quite certain that *your* offense is worse!"

Silence.

Then my question: "I know you need money. How much do you want? Of course you may realize that you are immediately sacked from my firm."

"Six thousand Marks and a few rings" was his down-to-earth answer.

"Within a week you will hear from my solicitor."

I closed the case and opened the door. My two protectors stood there. Their expression did not show if they had heard anything. The police sergeant opened the door and K. rushed out, to let off steam.

He ran to the street, stood there in his uniform, swung his fist toward the house, and yelled, "Lysol should be poured over the whole shack to clean it from the Jewish stink! But above all the Jewish breed should be extinguished! Come out, you damned Rebecca! Rebecca! Rebecca!"

It may have been the only name from the Bible he remembered. For a solid hour he repeated his curses and maledictions on the road in front of the house. Finally the police sergeant called headquarters in Mettmann. They sent a squad car to take away a sergeant who was molesting a war widow.

I began to search for a lawyer who was willing to handle a suit between an infuriated "Aryan" and a "Jewess." I knew that K. would be capable of denouncing a lawyer or notary who did something for a "Jewess," and that would mean that he would lose his license. I told my story to all the lawyers I knew. Nobody wanted to help me. Nobody could. It was too risky.

During a conversation with an old pensioned police prefect of Wuppertal, who was one of my egg customers and a firm anti-Nazi, I heard that his son was a lawyer. The old gentleman believed that his son would be willing to help me. That would be the case for his

Paul! The same night I met the lawyer in his parents' house and we drew up the suit. We also set up an appointment, when I would meet K. in his office. The lawyer was going to contact K. to make the appointment with him in time.

The following agreement was made:

1. K. had to keep quiet after the receipt of six thousand Marks—and two diamond rings. Neither he personally, nor a third party who had gotten the knowledge through him, would make use of my Jewish ancestry and hand me over to the Nazi officials. The agreement would last five years.
2. Reciprocally I would not sue K. for his threatening and punishable act of extortion, or ever ask for the return of the six thousand Marks and the jewelry.

We signed. I pushed six thousand-Mark notes across the table. Two beautiful family rings were on them. Like a card player K. threw the Hamburg photocopy on the table. Then he hastily picked up his new possessions and strutted out.

The lawyer asked me to take a seat. Comfortingly an unknown hand was placed on my shoulder.

I asked myself, Who would get the same Hamburg photocopy next?

Nobody did. Nobody anymore.

Before the five years of the settlement expired, the Nazi rule and the war were over.

———

In late autumn of 1943 we were all occupied in harvesting the last beans from the long sticks. While we were working, a large number of Allied planes flew past us and made a tremendous noise. We could not see them as they flew over the clouds. They rumbled like a moving van on a wooden bridge. I left the group in the garden and went into the house to turn on the radio, for the number of planes and their direction. As I stood in the room, a single bomb howled down and fell between the barn and the house. The pressure broke all the windows. Some whistling shrapnel passed close to my head and smashed into the wall. I ran to the window and yelled, "Everybody down on the ground! Lie flat!"

I went back to the radio. Nothing. Not even static. Nothing. Nothing at all.

The bomb, which was targeted for the railroad, had struck the main electric power line, and all electric lines in the whole district were destroyed. We stayed without current until long after the war.

Now the electrically heated incubators could not be used, and neither could the soup factory apparatus, which was vitally important in the general food sector. I could change one incubator over to petroleum, and I got a ration for it at once. The soup industry went on, with the help of our big copper wash kettle. The washing was done in a large tin tub put up on bricks in the courtyard. It all worked well after we had found a way.

The dark evenings had one advantage: nobody argued about my tiny candle. As the manager of a small factory, I got it on my ration, so that I could work at night. I needed it for all of us. After dinner everybody sat behind me while I worked. Then they went to bed early.

If only the radio still worked! I *had* to hear some news! Oskar had a small crystal set. I could not ask him for it, because he would certainly have asked why. He used it himself, and every night I peeled my son out of his entanglement in the wires; he used his bed as an antenna. After some time he just fell asleep and did not worry about further happenings.

In my room, I connected the small set to the long-defunct furnace. As always, I put a cushion on my lap, so that I could pull off the earphones and hide everything under the cushion if somebody came in. I knew I was being watched. The staff must have wondered what I had to listen to that late at night.

A lot.

All alone among "paid enemies," as friends used to call their employees, with the nerve-racking air raids on the Ruhr, at the rim of which my farm was situated, I had long listened to

"Big Brother": Churchill's speeches over the BBC. This powerful station spread general war news and addressed the German people, asking them to end the Nazis' senseless, hopeless war. I could follow it all on Oskar's small set.

Listening to such broadcasts was punished by being shot on the spot. But I did not listen to the news only for myself. Among the French prisoners at the Vohwinkel station were a few intellectuals, who were in contact with the French Maquis in the Ardennes. They asked Louis to have me get them news from Allied sources. They were waiting desperately for their liberation.

Louis continued to bring me one bucket of garbage twice a week. Very punctually he passed the garden before my lounge window and went into the farm's food shed, where I met him to empty his bucket. There I made him learn the latest London news by heart, and told him how to spell names for his fellow prisoners. He learned well.

From his descriptions I came to know all his comrades without ever having met them. We made an appointment for Louis to come during the night if there was an emergency and they needed help. Louis had cut a well-hidden hole in the camp fence and he knew the path through the forest as well as the road he took with his bucket.

For a year I had moved from the second-floor bedroom and me in 1942 after a total breakdown. Josette had promised to off, I did not move up again. I had arranged with the French prisoners that Louis would come to the house and whistle the V for Victory signal under my window. The others would not suspect anything, because his whistling sounded like the call of a small owl.

One night the "little owl" whistled under my window. Louis reported that his friends in the camp had dysentery and he asked for medicine. They were frightened that malnutrition would finish them off quickly. Things looked grim. I was glad I could help at once. I had sent Alex a large box of charcoal tablets. They had come back in the champagne box. With many good wishes for his comrades, I handed Louis the medicine.

He whistled happily when he passed my room with the bucket

the next time. The tablets had helped miraculously, he said. First looking around very carefully, to see if anybody could see him, he handed me an expression of thanks from all the prisoners: a tin of Nescafé. They all knew that women especially like coffee and after long negotiations they had decided to give me some!

Coffee—what a magical word! What an unknown enjoyment I had ahead of myself! For years we had been drinking a brown brew of roasted barley, which we called "pointed coffee beans." Some firms tried to improve it by adding other ingredients. This was the first Nescafé in my life, and it came from a French Red Cross parcel.

One night Louis arrived totally out of breath. From his confused reports, I gathered that one of his comrades had intended to brew himself some really good coffee. To be sure of it, he had poured a whole tin of Nescafé into an old pot and added some boiling water. He had then drunk the coffee with his breakfast.

Louis was absolutely desperate: *"Madame, Madame, il meurt! Son coeur bat comme fou! Je vous prie, vite, vite, donnez-moi une tablette qui tranquilise le coeur!"* ("Madame, he's dying! His heart's beating like mad! I beg you, quick, quick, give me a tablet to quiet his heart!")

I could help the coffee drinker calm his heart.

All happenings with the French were somehow touching. Once a lot of laundry hung over the lines in the garden. We could not wash our sheets very often, because our ration was only one packet of wash powder a month for five people.

Louis left the farm through a gate to the street. He suddenly stood as if he had grown roots. He took the corner of a sheet in his hand and petted it slowly: *"Des dentelles, Madame, des dentelles. . . ."*

He could not grasp it. During his rough years as a soldier, he had never seen lace.

"J'en suis sûr, Madame, que ma femme mettera les plus beaux draps sur notre lit, quand je retourne. Elle en a aussi avec des roses dans les coins. Et il y avait tant de roses sur l'oreiller,

sur ceux qu'elle a embrodée pour notre nuit de noce, que j'en avais toute la figure plein de roses le lendemain!" ("I'm sure, Madame, that my wife will put beautiful covers on my bed when I come back. She has some with roses in the corners. And there were so many roses that she embroidered for our wedding night that I seemed full of roses the next day!")

We looked in opposite directions, both with tears in our eyes.

One should not generalize. Certainly not. But there were times one could say that after 1943 the household help was not the best. After my last maid married a rabid SA man and I had gotten out of her sight, I had to get a new worker for my vital firm, because I could not manage without another woman to help me. How I would have loved some help!

A Mrs. Maria G. entered my service. She had been bombed out in Düsseldorf and preferred to work in the country.

Büscher, the old farmhand, who had been with me for six years, looked at me and growled, "You'd better look out with her, doctor! One only can look at the head of people, but what is in it may be pretty miserable!"

How right he was! One day we women sat in the kitchen, cleaning beans for preserves. My thoughts went their own way and I did not feel inclined to chat with Mrs. G. With much pride in her voice, she began to tell me that her husband was an SS police sergeant in Poland and that the Party, of which she was also a member, had placed her in my house as an observer, because I was known as a "politically unreliable person." She warned me herself. How right Büscher had been!

At the time that Mrs. G. entered my service, the goat Liese gave a lot of milk. I milked her myself three times a day and hid a small quantity of milk in a screw-lid jar in the shed. After dark I took the glass into the house and emptied it into a square container that had a small stirring mechanism attached to its lid. I could beat the milk with it. Once it had been a glove-cleaning device of Granny's. Her maid had cleaned her kid gloves in it with oil. Where were those times?

Butter making was forbidden. So I waited until late at night, when it was absolutely quiet in the house. Then I packed the small machine in numerous pillows to deaden the humming noise. In this way I managed to produce two teaspoons of unwashed goat butter for my children, which I gave as additional food value, sprinkled with sugar. But how did I know when Mrs. G. might come down in her slippers to take me by surprise? I decided not to make myself sick with worry.

After Mrs. G. had been in my house two weeks, she asked me for sheets for the large guest room, with its beautiful Empire-style shell-shaped beds. Her husband was coming on leave and they intended to spend this time in my place.

A week later the SS police sergeant arrived in the kitchen. He had a huge suitcase. He clicked his heels and saluted us with "Heil Hitler" to perfection. The couple went upstairs to the guest room and I sat down at my desk, waiting for things to come—and they did!

First Mrs. G. appeared in a magnificent coat of Siberian squirrel and played the mannequin before me. She then remarked that gray would not suit her gray hair. Wouldn't I exchange my Persian lamb coat for her squirrel? I did not answer.

At mealtime, G., the most wonderful of all men, came down to the kitchen. He had his right hand in his coat, Napoleon style, and moved it so that the large field police emblem on a chain around his neck clattered on his buttons. His existence was being rubbed in!

"We also need the kitchen!" G. demanded coolly. "I don't mind if you also cook and eat here, but I am not going to sit with you at the same table, and not with your staff either! I am something better! Come on, Büscher, get us another table, and from you, doctor, I demand a beautiful tablecloth!"

Fried potatoes were served at both tables. G.'s were cooked with bacon and lard. We had "pointed-bean coffee" in the frying pan and made fried potatoes "the Nazi way"—standing by the potatoes with lifted arm, which was supposed to make them brown. Then no fat was necessary!

The SS field gendarme came, with belt and pistol, for his meal. I knew that given half a chance, he would shoot. Büscher thought the same.

All went peacefully for a few days. Then the G.s were bored in our silent presence and began to show us their valuables from the heavy suitcase: radios, handwoven materials, colorful peasant embroideries. Whatever they proudly displayed, Büscher and I stayed silent. The children and the young girl did not speak either; they had learned to keep to themselves, as I did.

"You may wonder, doctor, how I get all this bacon, sausages, and other good things?" G. tried to get a conversation going. "As there haven't been any young men in Poland for a long time, as we have brought them to Germany for the war machine, we pick up some old men from the farmhouses and drive them to the arrest room of the field police. Then the whole family howls when we take the old ones away, and the women run behind our cars for some time, crying. We know that all. And when the evening comes and it gets dark, then the women come with baskets full of food they had hidden before and offer us all of it in exchange for the old men. They may have them back, but first the baskets are emptied and then we have our fun with the females on the guard beds! And when we have nothing good to eat anymore, the same starts again! What fun!"

G. could not stop laughing loudly. I saw how old Büscher put his fork down and how the knuckles of his fist became white. His moustache started to move critically under his nose. I had to calm him down. I got some of my own tobacco, obtained for him on my smoking coupon. That always helped.

"And then," G. continued, "we have a sport of our own. You may believe it or not, doctor. With this, my own pistol," and he hit it enthusiastically, "I once shot the mother of four, and the kids didn't even notice it. They were gleaning potatoes. *That* was a shot!"

Quietly and very slowly I got up from our table, took one of my children on each hand, left the kitchen, and sat down on the settee in my room. There I read them the tale of "Puss in Boots."

"Gleaning potatoes" is one of the most gruesome memories of the war and postwar times. After a farmer had emptied a potato patch, the field was given free to the people to pick over it once more. Many city people went to the country to get a little more food. They were not used to hard work and often collapsed in the fields. One of the most depressing and horrible sights of those years was to see old men, women, and children throw themselves unto the fields with their hoes, so many that there were only a few square yards to each one. It was desperately sad to see how luck gave one or another *one* potato, like a gift. At the corner of such fields were mounted police, to keep the group in order. If the people yelled, the police hit them with their tommy guns. Often there was blood.

I very well remember a dreadful happening on the neighboring farm: A young woman began to yell. A very old woman held a huge potato over her head. She had just dug it out with her bare hands. The young woman wanted the big potato for herself. The old one, who had found it, hung on. The young one yelled and fidgeted with her hoe. Two small howling children hung on her skirt. Before one of the policemen could gallop through the crowd, the young woman had lifted her hoe and banged it into the head of the old woman. She died instantly. She was driven away on a wagon. Her head rolled from side to side. One hand hung down the side of the cart. She no longer held the big potato.

This was called "gleaning potatoes."

It was the same with grainfields: After careful harvesting and raking, the fields were given free for gleaning. Only very little could be found. The grains were ground at home with a coffee grinder and eaten as porridge.

I remember a child, about six years old, who ran wildly around a large field opposite the house. His eyes were so full of tears that he hardly could see. He was afraid to go home, because he had found too little and feared a beating. I gave him my total bread ration for the next day: two slices of bread. I only drank warm water all the next day.

The following day a woman came to my door, begging for one slice of bread. She was starving, she said. I did not have any more bread. I went inside to look for something else. I found two cold boiled potatoes and an apple, which I intended to bring her. When I came to the door, the woman had fainted. Falling on the stairs, she had hit her head, which was bleeding profusely. She looked like my mother. For three days I nursed the unknown woman and gave her my rations. I had already gotten used to warm water. Then quietly and unnoticed the woman left. On the pillow of her bed I found a small brooch, which she had pinned there. It held a tiny photo of her son, when he was a child. She had left it with me as a gift. How I would have loved to return it to her! I have never seen the unknown woman again.

Mrs. G.'s stay came to an end. She told me that her health could not take the nightly air raids anymore. They would not let her sleep. The bombs, which now fell around our house constantly, were too much for her nerves. She wanted to join relatives in Thuringia and had asked for her evacuation there. I did not mind. She got the necessary papers and left.

For a long time the SS policeman G. had written to his wife every day, and she answered every day. So a number of letters arrived after Mrs. G.'s departure. Because I had her address I always forwarded her letters at once. One day a letter arrived, the envelope not sealed. The unknown in us, which cannot be held back, pushed me to read the letter.

After grasping its contents, I called for old Büscher, read the letter to him, and said, "Büscher, we both have to learn this by heart! I do not know whether these letters are numbered or somehow marked. If the letter gets 'lost,' anything could arouse G.'s suspicions. I do not want to keep it. That might mean a house search, and what would happen if the letter were found? We *have* to learn the contents by heart. Perhaps we may need to tell what the letter says!"

Today, nearly thirty years later, I still can recite the letter:

Dear Maria:
    You now have swept the dirt of this Jewess long enough. It is time that you save your life and join our relatives in Thuringia. After finishing this war victoriously, we shall take all we need from her house to furnish a nice flat for ourselves in Düsseldorf. And her, this doctor, we shall send there, where she will get out of a gas-chamber chimney the same way as her race mates. . . .

Old Büscher never became familiar. He had a certain mixture of respect and attachment toward me. Now he put his heavy hand on my shoulder and said, "Let her come to this farm once more, doctor, then I part her hair with an ax! Believe me, I shall!"

———

Mrs. G. was in such a hurry to leave that she forgot to inform the employment office. I was glad of this, because now nobody in Mettmann knew that I was without help in the house. So they did not try to supply me with another spy.

I had also recently sacked Alfred, the dwarf. He had tried to get Oskar into homosexual games with him. The child had told me of this approach and said, "I don't like anything like that, Mum!"

Now Büscher and I faced all the work, assisted only by a very young girl from the neighborhood. In the shed we talked about whether we could manage this way. I sat on the work-bench and straightened crooked nails with a hammer on a small anvil, to use them again. Büscher sat on the chopping block, smoking his pipe, the ax between his hands.

"You know, doctor, we are going toward winter and the outside work is easing off. I can give you a hand in the house as well. I shall look after the ovens, and in the evening I can peel a small bucket of potatoes. I shall also sweep the kitchen floor after the meals. I don't want any pay for these extras. What could I do with it? One cannot buy a thing. And I am quite certain that the old laundress will also give you a hand, if necessary. At least we know how she and her husband think politically. One can trust old Social Democrats, as they are. What about it, shall we try? I'm for it!"

My old laundress, who had my little suitcase, thought a winter without a spy, as she called it, an excellent idea. She was willing to help also. And so Christmas 1943 approached. We looked forward to it with spiritual peace.

———

Louis continued to come twice a week. He brought garbage and took the London news with him. When he heard that Mrs. G., of whom I had warned him, had fled and that Alfred, whom instinctively he never could stand, had left too, he said quick-wittedly, *"Alors nous allons célébrer Noël ensemble!"* ("Then we will have Christmas together!")

I had taken this as a casual remark and did not think about it anymore. Not so Louis. When he came the next time, he had worked out a plan in detail. He came with concrete proposals. He would bring five of his comrades along with him, passing through the forest after dark. The guard at their camp had already announced that he would be going home on Christmas Eve, if the prisoners were "good." To be "good" meant for him, Louis, to celebrate Christmas with Madame. If I agreed, he planned to bring the five oldest married men with him; they would miss their families most. He had already talked to his friends and they had inspected their hidden reserves from the Red Cross parcels under the floor of their shack. They decided to bring sardines as hors d'oeuvres and coffee to drink after dinner. Would I agree? Rather stunned, I admitted that it all was rather well thought out and organized, but I felt rather taken by surprise!

Büscher and I talked about the possibility of celebrating Christmas with the French prisoners. He thought it a splendid idea, especially because the little girl who had helped until then would be home for the holiday and would leave with the change of the year anyway. Büscher suggested that we roast our last gander and have it as a holiday meal: "Before it's stolen, we'd better eat it ourselves!"

In addition to the five French prisoners I had invited my dear friend Josette, born French, divorced German, and the old nurse Margarete from the Düsseldorfer Hospital; she had nursed me in 1942 after a total breakdown. Josette had promised to make a cake. For days, we saved the goat's milk for a pudding. So everybody had his task.

Büscher supplied a cleanly plucked gander, beautifully stuffed with apples. Josette and Margarete came in the afternoon to help me. We pulled out the kitchen table to the largest size possible and ransacked the ragbag for small pieces of material. We managed to find enough blue, white, and red bits to decorate the table with pine twigs and the French Tricolor. Nurse Margarete set the table and entertained the children, who burned pine needles on the kitchen stove until the air was filled with dense smoke! It would smell festive, they thought.

Then—a tremendous crash! On December 24, 1943, at 4:30 P.M. the Allies dropped a bomb between the railroad tracks and our house. The sheets of corrugated iron that had hung before the paneless windows were pushed in, as if by a huge fist. It was a lucky coincidence that the shutters were not closed at that time; they were the last help against the bitter cold of the winter.

Margarete and I ran into the locked room, where the Christmas gifts were to be given to each member of the party. The pretty Christmas tree, which Büscher had cut in my forest, had fallen on the crèche. The three candles, which Büscher had so laboriously melted together from tiny candle bits, were broken. The crèche figures were heavily damaged. They had been copied from an Italian crèche, plaster figures, hand-colored. The children had grown up with them and loved them dearly. I locked the room and promised distribution of presents for the next day.

The six French prisoners arrived exactly on time. They had dressed in brushed uniforms, wore ties, and had beautifully brushed hair, which gave them a festive look. Each of them presented himself, giving his name and shaking hands with everybody. Büscher said, "Good evening, comrade!" and honored each of them with a friendly pat on the shoulder.

We sat down at the table. Josette chatted and laughed, as only she could, while Margarete served the meal. The Frenchmen admired the plates and glasses, the silverware, and other luxuries they did not know anymore after years of life in camps behind wire fences.

The donated sardines did not meet with Oskar's approval: "What funny small fishes they are! Just enough to fill a hollow tooth!" was his judgment.

The gander was a great success. Potatoes and gravy were plentiful for all. The goat-milk pudding surrounded by preserved cherries was delicious. Josette's cake was served with black Red Cross Nescafé. We had wine. Büscher and I had dug out the first bottles since the beginning of the war, when I had buried all of them after Alex left to join the army. The last bottle of blackcurrant homemade liquor pleased everyone.

Music was requested. Büscher brought the old hand-wound phonograph into the kitchen. We heard dance and carnival music.

"Vous n'avez rien en français, Madame?" Louis asked.

Yes, I had one record in French. I did not remember where it came from: "Parlez-moi d'amour!"

This record put the Frenchmen off balance. They must have eaten too much, and the wine they had had to do without for years must have gone to their heads. Temperament and sentimentality took their toll. They thought of France, of their wives and children. They cried and, as a replacement, my children were petted and kissed. With funny, sweet-sour faces the children stood up to it all, but tried to wipe off the many strange tendernesses from their cheeks with the back of their hands.

Tears in her eyes, Josette danced with her compatriots.

Margarete clapped time with her hands. Gathered in a circle we sang the Marseillaise, holding each other's hands. Often and loudly Büscher blew his nose to cover up his emotion. What did I do? Every half hour I walked around the house with the Alsatian dog to see if somebody had climbed over the fence to listen. Then the Party might have been warned and the nest of traitors would be rooted out, a nest in their own country. One of us had to stay sober, and that was I, because I had the responsibility.

At 10:30 P.M. the French prisoners went home, weaving to and fro, extremely happy and satisfied. "Home" meant their camp of shacks between the railroad tracks of the Vohwinkel station.

Margarete washed up and Büscher dried the dishes. Josette and I treated the broken crèche figures with plasticine. They now all had brown hands; only the Moorish king had had them before. A thick round belt around their waists did not embellish them either. And so they stayed. A memory.

———

At the beginning of 1944 the food situation became even worse. The occupied countries were plundered. Nowhere could agriculture produce what was expected. Seed and fertilizer were missing. There was no fuel for the tractor motors and other machinery. Horses were requisitioned and the men were at the front. The population was hungry. Everybody was on his own and "organized" what he could for himself.

Outside the poultry farm fence I had a large field with rhubarb. Before the war I had sold the yield to preserve factories. Word of this field got around. Groups of city women came out by train and plundered as much as they could. In a way I did not mind at all, knowing myself how much hunger hurts. But I admit I would have preferred it if they had asked me for some rhubarb. I would have given it gladly, instead of having them clip it off wildly and damage the plants. But there was no good behavior anymore in a starvation year of a total war!

I went out once when I saw a woman, with two heavy bags

full of rhubarb, passing the house along the road. I asked her why she had taken more than she could use herself. I got a short and simple answer: "My husband died at Stalingrad. And I like rhubarb!"

My husband had also died at Stalingrad.

Before the war, there were no sheep on my farm. In autumn the village shepherd came with his big herd and grazed the meadows until the last corner was free of long grass. During the war, when it was permitted to keep a third of all wool produced by a sheep for one's own use, I bought English black-headed sheep, which were said to need little attention and could stand up to cold winters. Two-thirds of their wool had to be handed in for general use. The remainder provided stockings and pullovers for my children, both in very solid and rustic quality, knitted by my kind old laundress.

When I bought the sheep, I was told that they were permitted to be covered only by a purebred ram. "Nonsense!" said the old shepherd, in the autumn of 1943, when he once again grazed my meadows with his herd. "Forget about it, doctor. In spring I shall give you a ram for loan in return for all the grass I always get here."

And so he did. In the spring of 1944 my fifteen sheep had twenty-two lambs, a rather impressive performance and a very pretty sight. The children adored them and played with them. Some of the little animals were very attractive and had all shades of black, gray, and white. "Mum, the tiny lamb over there is mine!" Oskar called, "It looks so pretty mildewy!"

The great number of lambs under the flowering fruit trees looked very peaceful and gave us much pleasure. It did also to the highest-ranking official German sheep-breed inspector, who passed my farm in his office car. The official head of all sheep in Germany made his chauffeur stop before the house to ask me which wonderful stud ram had brought all the little sheep into this world. He would like to see the ram, he said. My staff answered truly: "We don't have any stud ram!"

The mighty official drove to the Gruiten city hall and denounced me for not following the stud laws. My disobedience was punished with a fine, and I was ordered to buy a stud ram at once!

I guessed that this high-ranking official would probably not pass my farm the next year, and so I again got a ram from my shepherd friend. After so many little sheep came again, a miserable old witchlike woman turned up. She lived in the Osterholz and everybody knew that she was spying for the Party. She came to ask me for the loan of my stud ram for her two sheep. Didn't I have one? "No," I said rudely. "I don't need one. I do it myself!" And I closed the door right before her nose.

One morning I looked into the farm to see where the sheep were grazing. The children ran happily toward the house and Oskar shouted, "Mum, today we are going to eat ram's tongue!"

Each child held a sheep's ear, which was "attached" to the head, as Alexa put it. The sheep pelt trailed behind. Only the head and the legs were left. During the night some soldiers from an antiaircraft battery had cut a hole in the fence and slaughtered the sheep. They had used colored wire to tie the legs together— wire such as only this unit used. Only the remains the children came along with were left, and some entrails near the forest.

I took the sheep's head and the wires to the city hall and asked them to take the animal off my inventory. The policeman returned with me to see my staff and ask whether the sheep had really been stolen, or whether it had been slaughtered without police permission. He heard what he needed to hear.

Three times a year an official checked the animal inventory on all farms. He went around and counted the animals himself. He was a correct and eager man, and neither alcohol nor a few eggs rolled into newspaper could influence him. When he came to my poultry farm, I had to lure more than a thousand fowls into their sheds with grain. Then the exit was made smaller with some bricks and the fowls were shushed out again. They came out one by one and could be counted. There could not be any error. The officials came unannounced on motorcycles, so it was impossible to hide any birds.

All people on the farm, family members as well as staff, had the egg production of 1.5 hen at their disposal, but of course they did not get egg coupons. (In the last year of the war, that was *one* egg per month!) On my farm there were usually five to seven people, so the unequal number of birds was rounded off. I had to show the feet of hens that had died, which were deducted from the inventory figure.

Because they were all breeders, I kept the sheds locked at night. They represented some value and were not just fowls. The windows of the sheds had heavy mesh wire. I knew the number of hens in every shed, which was surrounded by a meadow, and these were separated by high mesh fences.

Once, when I unlocked No. 5 shed early in the morning, no birds rushed out as usual. It was all quiet and empty. I can compliment the thieves' sarcastic sense of humor: Nicely executed on the first roost were the heads of twenty-three pedigree hens, all beaks pointing to the same side, and, in a marching distance, at the head position, the head of the pedigree cock.

"Mum," Lexa, who had followed me, asked, "can we also eat fowl tongues?"

―――――――――

If one has had a poultry farm for twelve years and during all that time has dealt with egg production, one is in a position to predict how many eggs should be laid the different months of a year. The normal production was much diminished because of the poor quality of laying flour in wartime and the small percentage of protein. Every egg of the farm was entered every night into a laying list, corresponding to the number the hen wore on a closed ring around her left leg. The number was written in pencil on the eggs in the laying shed.

Suddenly the number of eggs decreased tremendously without any reason. By coincidence my good laundress could help me. She was waiting at the tram stop. A child from her neighborhood joined her and started chatting: "We just can't stand eggs anymore! Mr. Hill, who lives with us and who now works for Dr. Wenzel, brings home so many eggs every day that we simply don't know what to do with them! We can't exchange them for anything else, or it would all come out!"

This report took my breath away. How could I catch the man? While the staff had their lunch, I went into the basement and searched the worker's jacket. It was stuffed with eggs. He went home after lunch every day. If I caught him on the estate, he could always say that he had found a nest in the hay somewhere and that he was just going to bring the eggs to the egg cellar, when the bell rang for the meal, and so he hung up his jacket with the eggs. He had to be caught outside the fence.

I took the car and drove to the police. I explained the situation to the official. He asked me to bring him to the first railway tunnel, which the worker had to pass on his way home. There he would stop and search him. I should wait and the rest would take place in my kitchen.

So I sat at my desk when the two men came down from the barn. The policeman held the chap by the jacket and pushed him forward. The sinner walked along with bent head and dangling arms. I waited for the two men in the kitchen, trying to control my laughter.

A scene followed that would have done honor to a circus magician. Eggs were taken from all pockets and put in a kitchen bowl, one after the other. There were twenty-three! At midday and in the evening the man had left the farm with certainly forty eggs per day, which meant four hundred in ten days! How could I not have noticed?

The egg thief was caught. I refused to have him punished. I had enemies enough around me. But two additional hands to help during the harvest were lost.

More and more overburdened with work, I had to try to get a bit more rest at night. My health could not stand so little sleep anymore. I decided to move the children with their beds from the second floor of the house to the basement. There they could continue sleeping, even during air raids, and for me it was no longer necessary to tear them out of their sleep at alarms, get them dressed, and take them down into the air raid shelter, which we had built in the basement. Büscher and I put their beds in the cellar between shelves with apples and stands with porcelain, Persian rugs, framed etchings, silverware, and other utensils that were in the way upstairs. Under the concrete stairs that connected the cellar with the kitchen was our contingent of potatoes, and on the other wall was a shelf with preserved fruit and vegetables. Jams and jellies also had their place there. The shelf was tied to the wall so as not to tumble over during bombardments.

The children thought it all very amusing. So they were taken out of my direct care. In the morning their hair smelled like the potatoes with which they had spent the night in the cellar.

11

The Fortress Without a Roof

Late in the autumn of 1944 every farm on the right side of the Rhine was ordered to take in the inhabitants of farms on the left side. The countryside there would be cleared and declared a war zone. This could happen only slowly, because the roads would be blocked. Such conglomerations of carts, people, and animals would attract low-flying planes. The officials had put my place down for six adults, two horses, and one cow. They knew that I could not put up the horses and the cow, but the farmer next door was willing to take a few more animals than he was supposed to.

On a Saturday afternoon in December, the village policeman came along on his bicycle to ask whether all was prepared to receive the refugees. Their arrival was expected the same night. Yes, all was prepared, I said. The rooms on the second floor and one of the attic rooms were at their disposal. There was no inspection. My answer was satisfactory.

It was very quiet and pitch-dark in the evening. Thick wet snowflakes were falling. The faraway barking of a dog sounded very close. I stood in wooden shoes at the big gate and looked toward the village. Our house was absolutely dark, and not even the outline could be seen against the forest. One lonely plane flew into our area. The beams of the antiaircraft searchlights hit hard against the clouds, which were heavy with snow and could not be pierced by the beams. The antiaircraft gun, which stood in our forest, barked short noises into the silence. Then it was quiet again and only thick flakes fell. There was nothing to be seen. I decided to go on waiting inside, because it was very cold.

Turning toward the house, by coincidence I saw a tiny, shaking light far away, near the barn. If we had been living in another world, I would have thought it was attached to a dog's neck. I stopped, more from curiosity than from the thought that it could be meant for me in any way. Soon the little light should arrive at the crossing, and then I would notice whether it moved down toward the village or up to my place.

It came up the road. After a short way uphill, it stopped, as though catching its breath. Then I heard a voice from the silence: "Everybody onto the spokes. Max can't make it anymore!"

Sharp horseshoes scratched on the asphalt, which did not give any hold. Heavy wheels screeched. I returned to the large gate and opened it. They should be my refugees.

Above two horse ears and two huge cartwheels I saw a huge cart approaching. I stepped aside and saw numerous bags, a stove, and some pieces of furniture, all tied down by heavy ropes. On the top of it all was a wooden crate with two geese, which poked their heads through the boards and made a tremendous noise.

"Welcome, welcome!" I said into the emptiness. I had not seen a human being yet.

Only after the second cart had halted on the road toward the house did a long old man lift himself from a cartwheel. He took off his hat, stretched out his hand and began: "Hassert," he said in a hoarse voice! "Are you Dr. Wenzel?"

I said yes.

"Would you allow us all to call our stay with you 'at home'? We have to wait here for the end of this terrible war. After that spell, we certainly will not have any home anymore. But it also may turn out differently. We were able to save all relics from our village church. They have been stuffed away in the safest corner, quite at the bottom of the second cart. I can already see now, dear lady, we will be able to get on well together!"

I gathered that old Hassert was a pious Catholic. Among Catholics, there were hardly any fanatical Nazis. I was also hoping for peace between the two families under my roof, I said.

While we stood in the yard behind the house, the other members of the Hassert family came along. They had followed the carts. An old uncle had his arm in a very primitive sling. I asked whether they had had an accident on the way. An old woman began to cry.

When I wanted to comfort her, old Hassert said, "Let her cry; she needs it. It will do her good. For such a long time she could not cry. And Karl, the fool, he had his arm too far in the spokes when the horse pulled on. But as Karl hadn't opened his mouth all day, it can't be too bad. Please let us empty the carts first, then we will look at that arm. Come on, Karl, hold the horse, or soon you will not have any arm anymore!"

I took old Mrs. Hassert with me into the kitchen, where it was nice and warm. After a cup of French Nescafé she perked up quickly. The efficiency of the three Hassert daughters and the strict command of the old man made it possible to empty the carts fast. One partition in the basement had been prepared for them, and all their goods went in. Then Hassert took the two horses by their heavy heads, the one-armed uncle led the cow by its halter, and they took their animals down to the neighboring farm. Later, when all six sat together in the warmth of the kitchen, they told me that they had a farm and a mill in the Düren area and that a small restaurant was added later. So they all had their work and what they needed. Some of the work had been a bit hard lately, but they intended to keep it all going until their two sons, who were on the Eastern Front, were home again.

We became friends. The women looked after their own household and spoiled my children no end. It was unbelievable what these many bags contained: potatoes, flour, carrots, bacon, ham, and preserves in tins. Every evening the children were given three walnuts each from the never-empty bag when they went up to say good night. There were also saucepans and porcelain, glasses and cutlery, and clothes, from fur coats to wooden shoes. So a complete new household developed under my roof, and we were all very happy to see how pretty and comfortable it was at Hassert's place!

The work of the four women circulated around the well-being of the old men. The doctor had had a good look at the arm and said that nothing was broken, and it healed fast. Only the coming bad weather tormented the old man. They were really old people: Mrs. Hassert was seventy-six, and the two old men were eighty-two and eighty.

So Christmas 1944 came closer. The postman brought a holiday gift to the Hassert family: a letter from the Eastern Front, telling them that their eldest son, a captain, would come on leave for Christmas.

Now some cooking and baking began. Much cleaning was done, and at long last there was singing! I had been asked whether they could erect a small chapel in the basement, which served as air raid shelter. The family intended to celebrate Christmas in their traditional way. The way to the Gruiten church was too far and too dangerous for them, with the low-flying enemy planes. So everything was ready for the arrival of their son and brother. The Hasserts had heard about heavy air raids in their Düren home area, but they did not intend to tell their son about the raids.

The Frenchmen understood that I could not invite them to share Christmas Eve with us this year, because I had other people in the house. But this made them very sad.

The time of waiting for Captain Hassert tied us still closer together. Though there were the bombs, the hunger, the cold, and the loneliness of the house near the forest, a festive atmosphere held us together.

The much-awaited son came home. For two days the Hasserts kept him in their rooms. Only the children had seen him. They said he was very much like his parents.

When he came down to see me, the captain humbly said, "Thanks is a very poor word, doctor. May the Lord bless you and yours!"

His deep feelings did not permit him to say more. He returned to his family upstairs. He was followed by my children, who had not had any school for a long time because the streets had been badly damaged by bombs and the hazard from low-flying planes was too great. The captain carved some fairy-tale animals from pine for them and made others from pine cones. He showed them the peasant art of the East and the old people watched him.

The three Hassert daughters and I continued to make war-Christmas biscuits and pricked out hearts, stars, moons, and little men from tough dough. And still they seemed the best biscuits ever!

On Christmas Eve I had invited the Hasserts to sing Christmas carols under our tree. The crèche was set up again. I told them of the damage the figures had suffered from the bomb the Christmas before. With a sad face Captain Hassert picked up one of the shepherds, who was embellished with two brown hands and a thick brown belt of plasticine. Very quietly he put the shepherd back among the others.

But our total war only began during the night in which a harassed world passed over the threshold between the years 1944 and 1945, during New Year's Eve.

Since the early morning of December 31, 1944, Allied squadrons had flown without stopping toward the east and northeast. Everybody had done his work and we all seemed tired and exhausted. It got dark and I put the children to bed early that evening. They enjoyed sleeping in the basement and told each other stories about mice, fairies, dwarfs, and butterflies, until they fell asleep.

The shutters had been lowered before the unpaned windows, to keep some cold out. If some close bombing occurred, they could be pulled up at once. Then it would quickly be cold again, because the corrugated iron sheets did not keep out the cold. For the last day of the year, and to give it a festive atmosphere, we had lighted the furnace to warm the house and dry it for once. It was very quiet in the Hasserts' part of the house. Büscher was resting on his bed which he had put up in the basement since the children were down there. He thought they were too young to be there on their own. On the last evening of 1944 I went outside and stood before the door, looking into a clear sky, full of stars. It was very cold indeed and also very quiet. No beam of light touched the sky. The world seemed to await the new year in peace.

Suddenly, with tremendous noise, the Allies flew in. All at once hundreds of antiaircraft lights raked the sky everywhere. And even more suddenly a number of "Christmas trees" hung around our house! The first bomb fell very close!

I ran into the house and called the Hasserts to run at once into the air raid shelter, while I went to pull up the shutters. Büscher came from the basement and helped me. When we arrived in the basement, where a tiny candle gave a pitiful little light, the children happily sat in their beds and thought in tremendous amusement that we had all come to see them. The Hassert women crouched in a corner and said prayers. Standing with closed eyes, Captain Hassert leaned against a wall.

The two old men were missing. I ran upstairs and called to them, as the bombs fell closer and closer. "What's the matter?" At last they came into the cellar. They blew their noses and sat down, absentmindedly looking at their hands. The house began to sway. One of the old men tumbled off his chair. We threw all the furniture out of the cellar and lay on the floor, because nobody could stand or sit anymore. I took command. Heavy, howling bombs came down. The ones that made that noise were called "Stalin's organs."

"Open your mouth! Fingers in your ears!" I yelled through the noise. A shell exploded. Very close. But—not *on* the house.

"I don't like that at all!" Lexa was quietly crying.

"Don't make any fuss, silly goat! We're not dead yet!" Oskar comforted his sister. Otherwise there was no speaking at all. The bombs fell and fell all around us. They weighed more than a ton each, and their explosive power was tremendous. We heard them fall. We felt the house shaking. The soil was frozen hard.

Everybody thought that the next bomb would kill us all. The bombardment seemed endless.

We lay on the floor for fifty minutes. The women prayed. The old men closed their eyes, as if they were sleeping. The captain had his head turned aside. I could not see his expression. Büscher smoked, lying down. I had my hands joined under my head and listened for every noise.

We lay like that for fifty minutes. For fifty minutes Büscher was swearing that they could look for other targets than peaceful private homes where anti-Nazis lived! What were they thinking. There were also two children among us—and—and. . . . Fifty minutes the bombardment lasted, and during this time the war year 1944 closed its eyes and the the war year 1945 opened its eyes, full of terror!

Then it was quiet, just as though one of the Norns had cut the life thread of the bombardment. It was absolutely still. The captain got up and brushed the dust from his uniform. Then he helped his old mother get up and, looking at me, said, "I admit I had no idea that the war back home was like *that!*"

Büscher and I went through the house. Shrugging our shoulders, we acknowledged that the last windowpanes had broken and lay in splinters on the floor, that some doors hung loose in their hinges, and other small details. But it was frightening that we could see the glittering stars through the roof! We and our friends had been tremendously delighted that the furnace had been on, so that we could greet the New Year in warmth and comfort—and now the safety pipes lay uncovered in the open. The outside temperature that night was six degrees! We realized at once that the insulation of these pipes was the only important job that had to be done. If the pipes froze, the boiler in the cellar could explode. And what then?

While we were talking about how to wrap straw around the pipes, I stepped out on a small balcony, where the winch hung, with which we could pull up bags with fowl grains and laying flour. A picture of horror was before me.

Büscher had stepped out also and stood beside me, remarking quietly "Zur Linden is burning. We both have to get there at once!

Let's get in our Wellingtons and run over! I'm certain the administrator and his wife have stayed at home, and what happened to all the animals, the many animals they have?" Horror made him breathless.

The neighboring farm in the direction of Vohwinkel may have been a mile and a half away, perhaps a bit farther. How long did it take us to get there? It seemed hours. We could not use the street, which was perforated by bombs. We walked, we ran across fields. Only in passing did we make some observations: The barn of Farmer Nix was no longer standing, and a part of the neighboring forest was in flames. There—another explosion, a time fuse! They could be everywhere!

An unknown dog came running and tried to bite into our boots. Büscher hit at him with his shovel. He had taken it with him to dig out the administrator couple, with whom he was friendly. There was a moment when I could not run anymore. I was out of breath in the cold. Büscher gave me his hand to hang on to.

Zur Linden's buildings were built around an inner court. The dwelling was toward the road. To this building, barns, stables, tool sheds, and other buildings were connected, and a large gate closed off the square. The gate was open. The burning rafters illuminated the large courtyard, in which two geese circled, blinded by the light, calling and hitting with their large wings. A foal also chased around, out of his mind with fright, not seeing the open gate. Otherwise there was nothing living to be seen. Standing at the gate, we called for the administrator. We could not get any farther; the tremendous heat made it impossible. We called again. No answer. We called together at the same time. Nothing.

There was nothing to be heard but mooing from the stable. Where once the pride of the farmer, his pure breed stable had stood, there was now only a heap of bricks and tiles. All the cattle were buried. They seemed to be calling for help. It was pitiable!

Büscher and I could not do anything. Extremely tired and

depressed, we slowly went home again. All the obstacles that had been difficult to overcome the first time, now seemed impossible! Our nerves began to give way. Tears began and could not be kept under control. I stopped and looked up to a clear sky full of stars, which stood imperturbably above me.

"There, take my handkerchief. You don't seem to have one, doctor!" I heard Büscher's rough voice talking to me. "I am afraid you soon will have an icicle on your nose from all the falling drops. Come on, the children are waiting. I'm certain they are all worrying about why we're staying so long!"

The children. Oh, yes, the children. They were probably standing in the attic to look out for us. It was a blessing for me that soon the gable of the house came into sight, so it was not so far anymore. We passed the small gate and walked toward the kitchen stairs. When we were nearly at the kitchen door, we saw the Frenchmen. There were Louis and his five friends, who had been our guests the Christmas before. They had heavy crowbars with them and looked like giants from prehistoric times.

I asked where they had been during the bombardment. In an old unused railway tunnel, I was told. All from the camp, all twenty-three? Yes, all of them. Then it became quiet. None of them looked at me anymore. They all looked silently in the same direction—toward Wuppertal, where a red sky showed the reflection of a giant fire.

The group had lost three men. Three comrades had left the camp too late. Shrapnel killed them while they were running toward the tunnel. The sheds took a direct hit. All their provisions went to hell! Who would ever believe that French comrades would be killed by Allied bombs? They wrapped the bodies in rags from their bedrolls, and the bodies were now in the camp kitchen, of which one wall was still standing. After having done their duty to their dead compatriots, they had started to walk to my place, to help us. To help us? I did not understand them.

Yes, they said, and pointed at their crowbars. They had stolen them a long time ago and hidden them in case we should be buried under our house.

"Oui," Louis said proudly. *"C'était tout préparé pour sauver Madame et les petits!"* ("Everything for saving Madame and the little ones was ready!")

The pressure of the uncertainty having gone, we embraced each other in the French way. Büscher rubbed his scrubby beard with his hands, full of embarrassment. After the sentimental wave was over, we returned to down-to-earth talk. Had the Frenchmen seen the administrator couple from Zur Linden? Yes, they had been in the same railway tunnel and had survived the bombardment. Soon after it began, a bomb fell on the water main before the tunnel entrance, and slowly, very slowly, the tunnel filled with water. The civilians had placed their children on their shoulders and stood up to their hips in ice-cold water. No one had drowned.

Now they were here, the Frenchmen pointed out. Their camp was absolutely flattened. Could I put them up somehow? I suggested the large fowl hall near the forest, which was full of hay. What a good idea, the Frenchmen thought. I saw them walking wearily, with hanging arms, toward the hall. There they turned on their heels and came running up again. A narrow bomb crater directly before the building could contain a time fuse! I decided to take them into the house, but asked them to wait awhile; I had a German officer with me.

Captain Hassert sat on a kitchen chair. He was bent forward and had his hands joined between his knees. He seemed to be far away with his thoughts and was rather startled when I began to talk to him.

"There are some French prisoners in uniform before the house, Captain Hassert," I began. "The camp in which they lived was totally destroyed by bombs. The group lost three men. These men came here with crowbars to dig out everybody who might be buried under this house. Also your family, captain, and yourself. As officer in my house I ask you for the permission to let these six men sleep in this house for one night—or what is left of it."

Captain Hassert got up. Slowly he opened the jacket of his uniform, with the ribbons. He hung it over a chair and placed it in a corner. Then he simply turned toward me and said, "Let them sleep in your house. We are all only human beings—and now I am no German officer anymore."

His old mother began to cry.

On tiptoe, like good children, the Frenchmen went into the cellar. I rolled out the Persian rugs, which had been on the apple shelves before the heat was turned on. Greedily the men drank a bottle of gin, which I had hidden for emergencies. They then stretched out and, dog-tired, fell asleep. They had survived the bombardment.

Two people probably did not sleep that night: Mother Hassert and I. The old woman, because she was worried about her younger son, Francis, from whom they had no mail for a long time, and I, asking myself time and time again how all this would end.

The following morning I found a leaflet on the farm. It had been dropped during the night. It read: "Fortress Europe has no roof."

Being shot was also the punishment for picking up and reading enemy leaflets. The impression this one left on me was so deep that I decided to keep it.

The report from Supreme Command told of a terror attack on Wuppertal-Vohwinkel and surroundings and said that 1,865 bombs had fallen between Vohwinkel and Gruiten. We certainly believed it.

The first day of 1945, after the horrid night we had had, we all spent in the attic: the old Hasserts, the captain in some of Büscher's work clothes, Büscher, and I. We were all up early. I let the Frenchmen sleep, but later they joined and helped us. We had turned off the furnace during the night and now we packed the pipes in straw. Then three French prisoners put the undamaged roof tiles in place again. After they had finished, we found out that a fourth of the roof was still untiled. With the help of the roof winch, new tiles were pulled up. Then we started to paint the concrete floor of the attic with big brushes and a paint we generally used to keep the rust off the mesh-wire fences, to keep dampness from the house, in case the roof was heavily damaged again. The atmosphere of a dozen people in the attic was excellent. Everybody was happy, because . . . we were all still alive!

In the kitchen the Hassert girls had cooked a huge pan of thick pea soup for fourteen people. Both families had given their share to it and the heavy meal suited everybody best after the hard work in the cold attic. Lexa got the order to get an apple for each member of the party from our cellar and had a little basket full of them when she returned to the table. She had chosen the most beautiful ones there were and somehow felt like Eve in Paradise handing them to all the men!

———

At the end of 1944 the German armed forces started a new attack against the advancing Allied forces. It was directed against France and entered history as the "Ardennes Offensive." Weapons and ammunition were stacked in the Osterholz, the forest behind our house, which stretched far into the Bergisches Land. All was organized from there to support the action. In my part of the forest there were camouflaged grenades, bombs, and ammunition, all stacked and numbered. Nobody was permitted to cross the forest without an official permit.

Probably Mosquito reconnaissance fliers had seen how worn out the roads from Vohwinkel and Gruiten to the Osterholz looked on an air photo. A large eight: and the farm and we were in the center of it. This position brought us the terror attack on New Year's Eve 1944.

The left side of the Rhine was now fully evacuated and was bombarded to create "scorched earth." What was left in the way of roads and bridges was now destroyed by low-flying planes. Slowly the war crossed to the right side of the Rhine. Even in Gruiten groups of Party members were formed, with the order to destroy bridges when the enemy approached.

By January 20, 1945, Captain Hassert had left us. A group arrived on the farm, driven at pistol point by some SA men, to defuse the bomb before the large fowl hall. Such an action was called "ascension command." They were Communists picked from concentration camps. Everybody who had defused twenty-five bombs of his own free will would be set free, so it was said. One of the men, a rope around his belly, was lowered by the others into the bomb crater and had to be very careful not to land with his foot on the fuse. He had to dismantle the bomb head and give a signal. Then he was pulled up again, with the explosive head. A specialist had to defuse the dangerous part.

It was a cold day and there was much snow. A low-flying Allied plane must have seen the group of people on the snow. It came down howling and shot into the poor chaps. Nobody was hurt. After work I invited the guards and the prisoners for a thick soup at lunchtime. I was told that it was forbidden to feed "dogs." I asked the SA men whether they would prefer to eat with all of us in the warm kitchen, or alone in the cold hall. They preferred the hall. I did not mind. Once again our soup was very much appreciated.

Since the heavy bombardment during New Year's Eve, the relationship between the French prisoners and their guards had become nearly human. Nobody was interested in these men anymore. Louis informed the guard that he would work on my farm and moved with Büscher into the basement. The Hasserts had given one of their rooms to the administrator of Zur Linden. They were only there to sleep, and meanwhile both worked hard to restore the damaged dwelling. Not a single head of cattle was alive after the debris had been cleared away. The frozen carcasses were pulled into bomb craters with tractors, where they would be buried. Before that, Russian displaced persons had boned the dead animals to the marrow. There were black spots on the snow where open fires had been lighted to roast the frozen meat.

When Captain Hassert left us, he said laconically, "You'd better build yourself a bomb-safe bunker in the forest, doctor! Perhaps you may be able to creep in there together when this all comes to an end. I heard that this part of the right side of the Rhine will also be evacuated."

The warning was meant for me alone. But Büscher had also heard it.

It was February 1945. Life continued, and nature did not hold its breath while the Western Front slowly broke down. Louis and I decided to trim the fruit trees together. He climbed into the well-kept high branches and I stood like a field marshal beside the tree and pointed with a long stick to the branches that had to be sawed off. We preferred days when the sky was not clear, because twice Louis had to let himself drop down from high branches while the machine-gun bullets whizzed around his ears. The Allies had tried to shoot him out of the trees. I am still sorry I was not able to memorize all the wonderfully juicy curses and insults.

The Allied forces advanced rapidly. We followed them on the map. German soldiers behind the front began to flow back. Some cars also passed on our road. They were mostly camouflaged and there were only a driver and an officer in them. The back was filled with suitcases and bags, all goods from France, which could be the basis for a new existence.

I kept all gates of the high fence locked, and only I could open them. My old Opel had served me well all through the war. I had been allowed to keep it for my vital food industry. I realized it would not be requisitioned if it was not in a usable condition. Büscher and I put it on wooden blocks in the garage and buried the wheels and tires under the peat shed, which was dry. I put the battery under my bed, and the distributor found a place in my desk. We owned bicycles, and the children thought it great fun to cycle with me when I went shopping.

Now the long-barreled guns shot over the Rhine. They had not hit us yet, but had already battered the villages around Düsseldorf. Again there was talk of evacuation to Wuppertal; we would be in it. I thought it advisable to bury all valuables in the house, because looting had begun.

It was a gray and foggy night that I chose for my plan. After midnight I put on an old gray coat with a matching cap and carried the family silver into the garden. I had placed a pick and a spade outside the evening before, near the round perennial bed, which was on the basement side of the road. I took a group of chrysanthemums out and placed them on the lawn. Then I dug a deep wide hole and put in the silver. I then threw the clumps of earth back. In my dreams I still hear the hollow noise of the soil falling on coffeepots and other items. It was very unpleasant. While I was digging, I could hear the detonations of the big guns. I stood there quite some time, leaned on the handle of my shovel, and listened to the end of the war coming nearer. But until it had rolled over us, a lot could happen. This was in March 1945.

Lexa and I were on our way to Vohwinkel to get bread, cycling along happily. It may have been ten A.M. Because it was cold, I had waited for the sun to have this excursion together. On the hill near Zur Linden we heard planes. Suddenly nose-diving, they approached us, not many. Everything moving, whether cars, locomotives, marching groups, or even horse carts, was attacked from a low altitude.

"Mum, Mum, now it's our turn!" the child cried and cycled faster, now downhill. I followed her and at the same time looked behind me. There were several of them, diving down on us.

"Get off your bike, fast!" I called to the child, who obeyed at once. We threw the bicycles aside and lay down in a gutter near the edge of the road. Fourteen Allied planes shot at us. I could see the men aim at us. The hits were very close. To shelter the child, I lay on her. Lexa cried bitterly and sobbed, "Mum, I wish Oskar was with us! Then at least we would all be dead together!"

Soon the aiming sport came to an end. It seemed to become boring to the fourteen planes. Shooting a woman and child had lost its charm. The first plane swung over the forest, and the others followed.

We brushed the dirt from our coats and continued cycling, because we had to get our bread ration. With my own coupon I bought a tiny cake for Alexa, or at least what was meant to be a cake.

"*That* tastes nice!" Lexa remarked. "If I could get another cake like this, I wouldn't mind them shooting at me again!"

Thanks. Not again. I was glad it was all over.

———

The retreating German soldiers began to take their provisions from German farms. This always happened at night. On March 31, 1945, two sheep were slaughtered in their sheds. The fattened ram followed on April 2; he had been earmarked for our own rations. I took the last three sheep into the furnace room. On April 3, the only cow was stolen from Farmer Nix. At the other neighbor's a calf was slaughtered the same night, and a few nights later all chickens disappeared from the miller's coop.

We constructed a Noah's Ark. The three sheep stayed in a wooden pen overnight. In another one were the goat Liese and her kid, Lotte. In still another one our pig, Cleopatra, lived happily, and from the once large poultry farm there were fifty hens and two pedigree cocks left. They shared the breeding cellar with one turkey and his four hens, as well as four geese and ten ducks. Except for the pig, all animals got outside during the day, and at night Büscher lured them back into the house with food. This was done by hitting the tin bucket. As soon as the animals heard that noise, they followed him into their boxes at once. Visitors who watched the maneuver from the terrace thought it was very funny. We did not think so, because danger was the deeper meaning of all these actions.

On the morning of April 12, 1945, a Frenchman came running to fetch Louis. They all had to report and stay in a temporary camp, surrounded by barbed wire. The Germans were afraid that somebody could run over to the Allies and give important information. It was a touching farewell from all of us when Louis left. He promised to return as soon as possible after his liberation.

On the same morning a group of military cars stopped before the small gate. Continuous tooting commanded me to open the gate. A high-ranking SS officer followed me into the house, opened all the doors on the ground floor, and, with a mighty voice, ordered the lounge cleared at once. He told me that he and his men were going to set up a mortar in the field opposite the house, to defend the Fatherland to the last. He was going to have his office in my room. Various SS men came out of the cars and were delighted that at long last the right position for the defense had been found. Everybody demonstrated his heroism by mighty orders. Everybody gave commands; nobody did a thing. I followed the scene, my hands in the pockets of my apron.

Soon afterward a grenade exploded, just where the mortar was meant to stand. With clicking heels and German salutes the heroes boarded their cars and looked for another place to defend the country.

But the day was not yet at an end.

After lunch a military motorbike stopped at the small gate and a single SS man demanded entrance. Swaying, he followed me into the kitchen, placed himself in the eating nook at the table, and stared into nowhere. I offered him a cup of war coffee and emphasized that I had no milk, because the goat was dry. He did not mind. He never took milk in his coffee, he murmured. Then he asked, "Would you mind if I defend myself from here?"

No answer from my side.

"Sit down here," the man continued. He took his field flask from his belt and poured a clear liquid into his coffee. Gin, I said to myself; that was the reason for his swaying.

"You know, I want to serve the Führer to the last, as he demands it from us. I am a member of the Werewolf, just so that you know."

Werewolf, Werewolf. It turned over and over in my head. I made a face like the bark of a tree. Rumor said this group was the most radical of all radicals and made it their task to be like revenging wolves. The thought crossed my mind. I had heard about them. Now one was sitting at my table.

He pulled out his pistol and put it at his side, to shoot every Jew, if one should come past, he said, now fully drunk. His eyes looked glassy and he stared at me. Oskar came in and started yelling when he saw the pistol. He thought his mother was being threatened. The child gave the man other ideas. He took a photograph out of his pocket. He explained that it showed his wife and small daughter. The woman was a real German Teutonic type, with long plaits around her head. Her white blouse was decorated with a brooch embossed with a Swastika. The little girl had long blond hair and held a small flag with a Swastika. I returned the photograph.

The man lost himself in the sight and began to cry again, "The Jews are our misery! I shall personally shoot each of them I come across! Now that they sniff some air of freedom, they will creep out of their hiding places, these pigs! I shall shoot them all! All of them I shall shoot for my Führer! I swear that I shall serve him to my last breath."

I had heard that before.

Now I thought that the moment had come for me to say something. I tried to explain to the drunkard that *one* man alone could not stop history and that gin was a bad drink for driving a motorbike. His sacrifice to the death would not serve his wife and little daughter. What they needed was a breadwinner after the war. I expressed everything very carefully. He probably did not understand a word. He was much too drunk, but my suggestion to try to find his military unit again, because he would not achieve anything on his own, seemed to sink in.

He swayed out of the kitchen. When he got out of the door and into the sun, he fell down the stairs headfirst and remained lying there. Büscher, whom I had called, helped him up, put him on his motorbike, and locked the gate behind him. Werewolf and motorbike went along the road for a few hundred yards. Then they both tipped over into the gutter. We did not care; we had to work.

During the night the first shrapnel from the long-barreled guns hit our roof. Early the next morning Büscher inspected the place where the Werewolf had fallen. He was not there anymore.

People had been cautioned to stay inside when the enemy approached. We were ordered to keep quiet, and house owners who flew a white flag could count on being shot on the spot. White flags meant unconditional surrender. The fight would go on to the last man.

My house near the forest could be seen from very far away. I could not run any risk, and I was not interested in getting into enemy artillery fire at the last moment. To be prepared for everything, the Hasserts, Büscher, and I talked things over. It was decided that the Hassert daughters would sew a bed sheet to a bean stick. It would all be hidden under the roof, if house searching was still going on. When other houses flew white flags, we would too.

On April 16 we were under direct shelling from 11:15 A.M. to 4:15 P.M. Oskar, with the eagerness of his twelve years, played a war game. He sat on the roof, near the chimney, and watched the position from a safe corner, with field glasses. It was not especially dangerous, but not risk-free either. A group of SS antiaircraft gunners were hidden in the forest behind the house and shot senselessly everywhere. Sometimes shrapnel hit our roof. None of us dared go to the farm. All the animals were still in the "Noah's Ark," and we sat in the sun near the garage.

We had cooked a lot in advance, and I remember that we had sauerkraut and pig's-feet, a dish that kept well without refrigeration. I called Oskar to come down and have lunch.

"Can't Büscher bring me a bowl of food up here? I don't want to smash a plate!" he called down.

"Come down, you fool, and eat something! We shall win this war also with you down here!" was Büscher's comment.

Oskar came down and climbed up again to his observation post, with a stomach full of sauerkraut. He soon reported, very excitedly, that he could see American tanks on the Haan-Vohwinkel road. He could easily make them out with the binoculars. We could not believe it and ran up to the attic. It was true. Tanks rolled along and nobody shot. They came from a direction where nobody had expected them. We talked about the idea of flying the white flag, but rejected it, because there was still shooting from the Osterholz.

The last night of uncertainty passed. It seemed very long indeed. There was no shooting anymore.

———

The next morning, Louis and three of his friends came to Gruiten and decided to settle in our dining room for good. They wanted to defend us against enemies of any description. They were heavily armed with German weapons they had taken from soldiers and were certain that some kind of shooting would start again soon. The stretch of forest that touched the farm had not yet been taken by the Americans and there was still danger for us, he said. I thought it was all rather exaggerated, but let them come.

We were again sitting at lunch, eating the rest of the sauerkraut with the Frenchmen, when American military vehicles rolled along our country road. They came from the Vohwinkel side. The Frenchmen jumped up and ran out. Full of astonishment and admiration they hung against the fence. Tears ran from their eyes. Slowly and rather dumbly we followed.

Then the children began to dance wildly. The Hasserts embraced each other and then me, and the three old men hit each other's shoulders.

The American tanks were followed by heavy vehicles, then antiaircraft guns. It seemed that a whole army was rolling along our narrow road.

Cigarettes were thrown over the fence by the Americans, who recognized the French uniforms. The Frenchmen caught them diligently: Camels, Lucky Strikes, Chesterfields.

Oskar stood very close to the fence, absolutely fascinated. Then he turned to me and asked, "Mum, the black man at the steering wheel, is he a Negro?"

I said yes.

"No, Mum, I don't believe you. That's not correct. He's not. We learned in school that Negroes always have bush knives between their teeth. And he doesn't."

What could I say? He should know.

Our thirty years' war, as Granny once wrote, had come to an end.

Yet, though military action was over in our area, another war began, a small war, the scale of which we did not know yet, but which was even more crushing.

The great Allied offensive from the west advanced with British armies north of the industrial centers in the direction of Hamburg. The American armies went forward in the south, toward Berlin. This pincer movement caught several German armies and twelve million displaced persons, workers for Hitler's war machine from all parts of Europe. We were included in this group.

Our area was occupied by Americans, who made Mettmann their headquarters. In addition there was an Allied headquarters in Hilden, where liaison officers from all former German occupied countries had their offices. From here the slave labor camps were dissolved and the prisoners repatriated.

Many German soldiers caught in this area tried to walk to

their home towns. They attempted to get civilian clothes from the population and threw their uniforms away. They also threw away their guns and ammunition. The big ammo dump in the Osterholz was unguarded and every displaced person could take whatever he wanted.

The German army walked unarmed on all streets. The soldiers in civilian clothes had their paybooks in their pockets, but no discharge papers. It was a tremendous snafu!

While the German army became civilian nomads, the forced laborers donned uniforms and armed themselves as heavily as they could. The first Allied troops could not keep them in their camps; they had been there too long already! They rejected camp food; they wanted the meat they had been without so long.

At the same time the German civilian population was asked to hand over weapons, field glasses, and cameras. American soldiers were permitted to search houses at any time. We had to bring all we had in that line to the Gruiten city hall and got a receipt. So we stood weaponless against the armed hordes. Now we saw that Louis was right in moving into our house with his friends to defend us. He was waiting for a time when we needed his protection.

The looting began. The foreigners got food for themselves, but nobody was shot in our district. The persecution from those who had been kept in camps for so long did not reach the point we had expected. I can only praise them, but, where there *was* real plundering, the people did not have an easy time!

The Americans, on the other hand, tried to satisfy their collecting instincts. The most searched-for souvenir was the old army revolver Type 98. One or two cartons of cigarettes were given for such a find, a small fortune on the German black market.

Meanwhile I had reassembled my Opel. As a now "reliable person," I got permission to drive the car for four miles around the farm. I also got two gallons of gasoline per month. Because I belonged to the food sector, I had a big green sticker on the windshield.

When I came home one day, I found four American soldiers in the hall. They were admiring the large Swastika flag the

Party had ordered me to buy. They had found it in the bookcase, where I had forgotten it.

"Are you a Nazi?" I was asked. Horrified, I said no! But the flag? I told them my story and my fate. They were astonished. Could they have the flag as a souvenir? With pleasure! The sooner it got out of the house the better!

———————

Meanwhile the Frenchmen had settled in the dining room; its windows looked on to the road. They preferred mattresses on the floor to beds. They lowered the shutters to the height of one hand and placed their guns, loaded, but with the safety on, against the windowsill. For the safety of the children, they kept the room locked.

We arranged that I should wake them up if I heard something suspicious, so that they could repel any attack. The Frenchmen were always tired and slept well. They just could not believe that they not only had real mattresses, but also blankets, feather pillows, and sheets, and that they could look up to an undestroyed whitewashed ceiling!

One night I woke up from my light war sleep. I had heard a strange noise. I went to the kitchen window, which opened to the forest. It had iron rails, but no windowpanes. The fruit trees were in full bloom and the full moon made them look like bunches of flowers in the meadows. It was a very peaceful sight. Suddenly my children's small black Pomeranian, which had its hut under the kitchen and which was on a chain, started barking fiercely.

I saw four men coming over the meadows, approaching the house. Each one held a gun over his shoulder in the military way. When the men had come within twelve feet of the house, they began to cut a hole in the fence. Out of the blue I yelled from my kitchen window, "Get out at once!" Rarely in my life have I seen men run away as fast as they did!

My yelling woke the Frenchmen, who came into the kitchen with their guns. The intruders were already out of reach on the edge of the forest. One of the Frenchmen placed his gun in the window and pulled the trigger. The shot echoed from the quarry. The echo had hardly faded, when one shot was returned from the forest. So they too had had ammunition.

"Mum, are you dead?" Oskar asked, coming up from the basement with a crying voice and a sleepy look.

I was not dead, but I was very very tired.

This was the first attempt at looting. Others followed. They seemed to be the order of the day.

The Frenchmen who stayed with us had to report regularly to the American officials and had to pick up their rations at American headquarters. This took so long that they went in two groups, so that two men could always be at home to guard us. The Frenchmen put their rations on the kitchen table, for all of us. They gave the children all the candy they got. The American provisions were packed in beautiful papers and tins. We had not seen such things for a long time. They gave us much pleasure.

It was therefore rather unpleasant to see two Frenchmen enter the kitchen one day with a huge piece of meat knotted into their dirty handkerchiefs. The blood dropped on the tiled floor. Before I could ask where the meat had come from, I was told that a crowd of hungry people had divided a horse between them. This was a piece of it, and the fat was also in the parcel. Would I please fry it for them? They felt like having an enormous horse steak. Rather flabbergasted, I asked whether they wanted it at once. Yes, at once.

As persuasively as possible, I tried to explain to my French friends that fresh horsemeat was not healthy; it would cause diarrhea and other ailments. I asked if I could leave the meat in vinegar for one night. In vain. The greed for meat was such that no brainwork could influence it. Even my suggestion of eating some bread with the meat was rejected. They wanted to eat *meat* and nothing else! So I was forced to fry huge horse steaks and serve them. The children got tiny bits. I did not allow them more.

Oskar had some army bread with his. Lexa poked around in her meat. She did not like it.

I prefer not to talk about the results of that meal! But the Frenchmen learned that fresh horsemeat does not do anybody any good.

———

Then came the spring day in 1945 when all four Frenchmen had to report at the same time to their liaison officer. All former French prisoners were to be divided into groups, according to the Département they came from; they would soon return to France. They gave me the good news joyfully. Now everything would soon be over. How glad they all were!

About midday, after all the Frenchmen had left, I heard a constant knocking at the kitchen door. Through a gap in the curtain and the fencing on the door, which also had no panes, I looked outside and saw four daring-looking figures standing outside. They were armed, and one of them fumbled around with a revolver when he saw me. With his left hand he made a sign around the house and asked me to leave the kitchen and go with them. I stepped out and closed the door behind me. When we were on the farm, one of them—they were Russians—lifted a forefinger and made a noise like "An CH, an CH, an CH!"

I felt pretty miserable and thought of our only pig under the house in the basement, which was due to feed us instead of rations for a whole year.

The other chap continued fumbling with his revolver and pointed excitedly and enthusiastically to our very last gander. He danced from one leg to the other and repeated, "CH! CH! CH!"

A gander was at least less than a pig. So I took a long hook from fence wire and swiftly looped it around the gander's legs. With one leg gone, the bird fell on the grass and I could easily pull it toward me. To display his admiration for that kind of gander catching, the Russian held his revolver high over his head and fired. It looked tremendously dangerous. He closed his eyes in fear of the shot and pulled his head down between his shoulders. Nothing happened. There was no shot, no detonation.

With my left hand I held the gander by the legs. With my right hand I demanded the revolver, which the idiotic chap handed over to me at once. I turned the cylinder with my thumb. It was empty. Then I placed his own revolver on the Russian's chest and tried with many gestures and much wild talk to make it clear that I would denounce him to the Americans, if he ever set foot on my farm again and that the Amis would make bum-bum and shoot him. He seemed to grasp what I said.

Then I pulled the trigger on his chest. He almost keeled over in fear. I handed the gander to the two men who had come with me to the farm and returned to the house. Büscher and the children had watched the happening from the kitchen window.

When Oskar later talked about it all, he called the scene "Mum under Russian revolver" and thought it was all wonderful!

When the Frenchmen returned from Vohwinkel, they went to their room to begin their preparations for leaving. Shortly afterward they all stood absolutely disturbed before me in the kitchen. They held a small cardboard suitcase! They cried the desperate angry tears of men to whom bitter injustice has been done. While two of the Russians had gone with me to get the gander, the other two, without Büscher and the children having noticed anything, had climbed into the dining room. With the butts of their muskets they had forced the shutters open. Then they had entered and cut the suitcase open with a sharp knife. They had looted it. It had contained the wedding rings, watches, papers, and last belongings of the Frenchmen's dead comrades, who had lost their lives during the heavy bombardment on New Year's Eve. Now everything was gone.

Heavily armed and full of rage the Frenchmen ran after the Russians. But it was too late. They returned empty-handed.

A few days later our French friends left us, to return to their homeland. My gratitude went with them.

12

Meetings and Decisions

Life continued without the Frenchmen, and what it demanded from everybody continued also. Eternal and unchangeable, a beautiful spring followed the cold winter, and, as a source of every kind of reflection, garden work reentered the daily routine. It seemed as if the soil pulled the abundance of grief out of me and left only the maximum bearable weight on my shoulders. Perhaps I still clung to a thread of hope that one of my people might return. This kept me going. Hope never dies, as long as you don't hold an officially stamped paper with facts. Only then does the thread of hope break, and the hard fall into reality is terrible!

A thick line finished the war diaries. Now the notes about daily happenings could be put in a few lines. Life had not become normal yet, but it was much more bearable.

Rapt in thoughts of my family, once again I worked in the vegetable garden near the road. A very old couple was struggling to pull a handcart uphill toward Vohwinkel. Their hair was disheveled and their clothes were very ragged. When they saw me, they stopped and wiped the sweat from their faces. I offered to get them something to drink, but they declined. They only wanted to stop a moment to catch their breath. On top of many old boxes and cases was a bird cage with a parrot in it.

We started talking. The old people told me that they had been evacuated near the Neandertal. They had survived the end of the war there and now wanted to fix up their little garden shed, in which they had lived before. If they did not return the few things that had survived the last attack on Wuppertal would be stolen.

While we talked, the parrot turned his head from side to side. He hopped back and forth on his perch, asking for attention. He also croaked a bit, as though trying to say he wanted to get on with the trip!

"Our Polly is already more than a hundred years old," the old woman began. "I got him from my grandmother, and he is like a child in the house. Come on, Jack, scratch his head a bit!"

The old man shuffled around the cart. He poked his fingers through the bars and did as he was told. The parrot turned happily under the scratching. Then he suddenly hopped to the middle of his perch, looked to heaven with one eye, and croaked happily, "Heil Hitler! Heil Hitler! Heil Hitler!"

Speechless and desperate the old people looked at me.

"Can't you tell me how we can keep Polly from greeting everybody the Nazi way?" the old woman asked.

I did not know how, I had to admit. The old people got back in the towropes, which made their work easier, and began to pull their handcart farther. The parrot hung on the side of his cage and tried to get at an old reed chair, which he had already practically pulled to pieces.

The old chair on the cart reminded me of a chair that Vincent van Gogh had painted several times. At the beginning of this century one of these chair portraits had been offered to Granny for about twenty-five dollars. She did not buy it. She thought it was too ugly.

———

In the kitchen, from where one could look towards the street, I heard the constant tooting of a car. The gates were locked. When I went out to see what the constant noise was about, I found an American military vehicle. An officer and a civilian were getting out of it. I unlocked the gate and invited the two gentlemen into the house. They wanted to ask me a favor, as the civilian called it. First the civilian and I talked in German about war problems. I spoke very shyly, not being used to free speech. While we talked, I looked at the American in military uniform. He was gazing at the pattern on a Persian rug. I noticed "POLAND" on the sleeve of his battle jacket. He held his steel helmet between his hands.

Suddenly he addressed me in English: "That's a beautiful Persian rug you have here, Madam, a Senné. I once had one like it. 'Once' means before the war, in Poland."

And so we touched a personal interest. I made coffee. The officer offered me a cigarette, which I declined. I handed his cigarette case to the civilian. The officer tried our homemade black-currant liquor. He asked where I had learned English and wondered if he might hear something about me.

I told the officer that I had lost my family because of the Nazi racial laws, and that my husband had been killed in the war. But I was still hoping that somebody would come back.

"I'm sorry, Madam," the officer said very quietly and pensively. He went on: "My own story is just as sad. I'll tell you about it another time. My office is in the American headquarters in Hilden. I'm a lawyer. I'm in charge of the problems of all Polish displaced persons. Excuse us for leaving now, but I have to be back in time for a conference."

The civilian told me why they came. At one of my neighbors the officer had traded in a bottle of gin, and now they were going to ask me for a couple of eggs, to make an egg liquor. The officer seemed embarrassed about this demand. He started toward the door. I went into the basement to see what I could give away. I handed the civilian a tiny bag with two eggs. Some ridiculous idea made me put one egg in the officer's helmet. I said, "So that you won't go without something!"

"Many thanks, Madam. I intended to ask you for something else: one red rose."

How often had I seen Granny cut red roses as a gift for

visitors, I asked myself as I cut three of them for the captain.

"Do you realize that I've already known you a long time?" the officer asked me near the gate. I looked at him. How could that be?

"Do you remember the day your neighbor offered you some 'Polish pigs' as workers after the end of the war in Poland? Do you remember that you rejected the offer for humane reasons? Among the prisoners were two who understood German and were in contact with a Polish underground group in the Rhineland. At that time your name appeared in a list of 'reliable people.' I knew as much as that about you when we came in. My friend's idea to get some eggs corresponded exactly with my wish to meet you. I am extremely glad to have made your acquaintance, Madam. I hope we will meet again."

They left. I felt a slight shudder between my shoulder blades. How fine all those threads were spun, of which we knew nothing.

From the small gate to the house the path was lined with rose bushes on both sides. I had planted more than a hundred there, after collecting exceptional species in horticultural exhibitions or at special gardeners. They were my pride and I always cut them myself. Every night after finishing my work, I passed among them with Granny's flat flower basket and cut the faded ones. I have often been teased by friends who said that my roses were ridiculously close to my heart and that they never had seen a petal on the ground under a rose bush. This was my hour of contemplation, when the sun sank and I was alone before the house in the fading light.

At this time of the day the Polish officer who had introduced himself as the Polish legal liaison officer stood again at the small gate. He asked permission to come in. He had a briefcase under his arm. I asked him to come in for a cup of coffee. Before I could make it, he took out a sheet of paper, which was narrowly covered by typewritten lines. He told me that, as a racially persecuted person under the Nazi regime, I was now under the protection of the army of occupation. He had looked up the legal side of my problems and here it all was in black and white:

Supreme Headquarters Allied Expeditionary Forces,
18th November 1944
    Administrative Memorandum Number: 39
        II. United Nations Displaced Person.
            9. Responsibilities.
                a. Responsibilities of Commanders.
                    (12) Assist in protection of United Nations displaced persons and their property, rights and claims.
            14. Procedure for dealing with special cases.
                f. Neutral displaced persons, stateless persons and persons *persecuted because of their race, religion or activities in favor of the United Nations, including persons of German origin.* The above will be accorded the same assistance granted to United Nations displaced persons, provided that their loyalty to the Allies has been determined.

After having read it all and grasped its meaning, I looked out into the night, which lay before my window.

"I'm sorry I can't do more for you," the officer said. "As an officially stamped paper, it may be of use to you. That's why I brought it along. May I tell my story in brief? You may then understand that your fate touched me deeply. My father was President of the University of Warsaw. We were ten children, five brothers and five sisters. Nobody would have believed that my small Hungarian mother could have given birth to ten children! During the First World War, two of my brothers, a surgeon and a Catholic minister, were deported by the Germans, and two of my sisters were shot. During the Second World War, in which I participated from the first day, from El Alamein to the Normandy landing, I again lost two brothers and two sisters. The Nazis shot them for being members of the national Polish underground group. My young wife and my baby were chased into the cold of a Polish winter by SS men, and they froze to death. I also hang on that thin thread of hope, as you call it, to see my old mother and my youngest sister once again. They are also probably hanging on the same thread. That's my story in a nutshell, as one so rightly calls it. May I ask you if I may leave now, Madam? I am afraid otherwise I may become sentimental."

I accompanied the captain to the small gate. A tiny flashlight he had taken from his briefcase shot its beam over the roses near the entrance. It stopped over one red rose. I broke it off and handed it to him. We did not say anything else.

I locked the small gate behind the Pole and watched the headlights of his car disappear over the hill.

On June 18, 1945, I wrote in my diary: "A meeting came to an end. . . ."

Meanwhile the Allied forces had built temporary bridges over the Rhine. The evacuated farmers from the left side of the river were ordered to return to their homes. They were also ordered to rebuild their destroyed houses and to try to work their devastated fields again.

So the day also came that the Hasserts pulled their two carts from the barn, harnessed their old horses, and began to pack their belongings. Because all the food had been eaten, there was more space on the carts now, and the three old people could make the long trip to Düren on top of the carts.

The farewell was just as hard for those who stayed in Gruiten as for those who returned to their totally destroyed home. Through the hard years we had tried to ease one another's lives. We had become a unity. Now we had to separate again into two groups. It was a deep wound which hurt badly.

The reciprocal gratitude remained. We still saw each other, while a new generation grew up.

In the course of the most vital reconstruction of the Rhine-land, the electric power lines were rebuilt. The waterways and canals were put in order again. Locomotives, railroad cars, and tracks were repaired. American military engineers built more bridges over the Rhine, and six months after the end of the war, the first trains from Wuppertal to Cologne and from Wuppertal to Düsseldorf were running again. To get to Cologne, one had to leave the train at Cologne/Deutz and then walk over the pontoon bridge. The old railway bridge over the Rhine had been destroyed, and had to be rebuilt to carry the train traffic.

I had to go to Cologne on business. I left my car at the Vohwinkel station and boarded one of those postwar railroad cars without windowpanes. It was cold and drafty. The train was overcrowded and I stood in the corridor.

Beside me, clad in the well-known leather coats without epaulets and SS insignia on their collars, were two young men in their late twenties. The train passed a totally bombed-out factory. All the passengers solemnly took in this picture of devastation. Then one of the leathercoats said, "This all happened thanks to the Jews! We haven't killed enough of them yet!"

Times of self-control for me were past. I took off my glove and there was a red mark of my hand a moment later on the cheek of the man who had made that remark.

From all passengers iron silence crept up to me. An older gentleman quietly took his visiting card from his wallet and handed it to me. "In case you need a witness, Madam!"

I took my visiting card from my handbag and handed it to the man I had hit, so that he could denounce me if he wanted to. He preferred to crush it in his hand. Then he threw it out the window.

At the next station, I changed to another car.

Now the "denazification" comedy started. As a now "reliable person," I had been asked to work as an interpreter for the occupation army. Because I knew English and French, I was asked to help with the papers for our village. For six weeks I tried hard to fit into that work and do it objectively. Then I gave up in disgust. Nobody there had ever been a Nazi, and nobody had harmed anyone else. They had all been forced into their deeds. They had gotten orders and obeyed.

All officials were dealt with leniently. I remembered something Granny had once said: "The Germans are not a revolutionary people like the French, Gertrud. They are born with blind obedience. A young officer once explained how that would work out. His example stuck in my mind. I'm going to describe it to you: A building had to be stormed in a military exercise. The soldiers put up their bayonets and started running toward their goal. Suddenly a sergeant started yelling, 'Don't step on the lawn!' And they all stayed put!"

Every Nazi stood in a pool of amiability, kindness, smiles, and self-consciousness. After the officials were investigated, the general population was asked to get their denazification. Some people were said to have some "brown," meaning that the color of the Nazi shirts rubbed off on the people who wore them. These people tried to get that color washed off. They took measures to contact a "reliable person" to obtain a "Persil ticket," meaning being cleared, as when washed with Persil—so-called for a German brand name detergent.

A number of people from Gruiten approached me for such a whitewash ticket. Among them was one of my more distant neighbors. He had belonged to the SA horse brigade. The owner of a factory, he had done well during the war. He had never been in my house. I asked him in. After hearing what he wanted, I turned him down flat.

"But why, doctor?" he had the courage to ask. "I have never done you a bad turn!"

I explained to this gentleman that he had never done me a bad turn because he had never been ordered to. If he had, he would have snapped to attention. Later, he would have reported to the Gestapo that he had obeyed the order. I thought of the millions of murdered people, and of my family. I would not even *think* of giving him a whitewash ticket. If I did, I would be sanctioning their deaths.

He left.

A few weeks later, the same gentleman stood at my door again. He had marched through the gate, whistling happily. I had seen him coming as I worked in the vegetable garden.

Without greeting me, and without any introduction, he said, "Listen, doctor, if I had known how easy it is to get the denazification papers, I would not have given it a thought! I would also have saved myself the walk up here to see you, and it would not have been necessary for me to listen to all the nonsense you threw at me!"

That was what he said. He left without another word.

———

With the trains running again, the mail also began to arrive. With this, the hope got stronger that I would get a letter from those who had been missing so long.

The first letter of horror came from the Dutch minister who had so kindly looked after Granny and Aunt Betty in Arnheim. The letter had gone to an aunt of mine in London, who had forwarded it.

Translation of the letter addressed to Granny's niece, who sent it to me after the German mail service had been restored:

Arnheim, June 22, 1945

Eglise Wallonne
d' Arnheim
Pasteur J. F. Hayet

Dear Madam:

I just received your letter with the first batch of mail handed out since September 16, 1944. Please excuse my use of this paper; I owned about 100 writing tablets which were stolen by the Germans, only two remained, and the hole is a gift of the British—it was created by the splinter of a grenade.

In view of the warm friendship which we felt for your mother, we did everything humanly possible for your relatives, and we became good friends. Your aunt (Granny) was very amiable and prepared to follow our advice after having comprehended its soundness. Your cousin (Betty) was emaciated and very nervous and excitable. She changed her decisions from one moment to the next, which made our efforts difficult, and often pointless. It was a consequence of her anxiety and illness. But as painful as our worries about the Jewish problem were, we had very pleasant afternoons and evenings together.

After their expulsion from The Hague, I advised them to hide in a small country village. This was in the autumn of 1940. *The Germans had not yet succeeded in arrogating the entire administration of the country to themselves.* They (the two ladies) refused because of a fear to be bored by life among peasants. This was a *very great* mistake. Then the Germans demanded that the Jews turn in their money and jewelry at a single bank. This they (the two ladies) did against our advice. Second mistake. Then the Germans decreed that the Jews register and carry the Yellow Star. This, too, was done against our advice. Third mistake—and an almost incorrigible one, for from this moment on they came under the direct surveillance of the SS and the Gestapo. However, it was not yet a completely lost cause. Upon the decree forbidding Jews to live in hotels and pensions, I founded a committee of friends. They undertook *the obligation* to donate all the money and food necessary to keep your relatives alive *till the end of the war* and to provide hiding places for them. Again, they failed to accept the suggestion—this time, however, because they did not want our lives to be endangered.

In the autumn of 1942 began the raids against the Jews in Amsterdam. In the winter of 1942 they (the two ladies) would have preferred taking their own lives to being deported. I dissuaded them. Once more I insisted *in vain* that they hide in the countryside. There were still faraway places (Drenthe, Achterhoek) *never* set foot on by the Germans.

In the spring of 1943 the deportation threat became more serious. Many Jews had managed to get to Switzerland; they had bought the help of German policemen. I advised them (the two ladies) to do likewise, but again without success, owing to the unreasonable refusal of your cousin (Betty). For your aunt (Granny) accepted my proposal to sell her pictures and silver at auctions—prices had skyrocketed, one teaspoon brought as much as ten Gulden. She was prepared to join a group of Jews planning to move together to Switzerland. A few weeks later, the management of ENKA (A.K.U.), the big silk factory in Arnheim (whose director general, deputy chief engineer and influential founder I know personally), brought together seventeen Jews who were to be sent to Switzerland by the ENKA. The ransom to be paid to German policemen amounted to 6,000 or 8,000 Gulden per head. They (the two ladies) refused to join. Two or three weeks later we heard that the entire group had safely arrived in Switzerland—German military vehicles had carried them across Belgium and France! Now they (the two ladies) decided to say yes! But now it was too late—that group of seventeen Jews had been the last one able to leave Arnheim. I deeply regret that all our efforts, made under danger to our own lives, were so sadly rendered fruitless by the nervousness of your cousin (Betty). Had your aunt (Granny) been here alone, we could have hidden and thus saved her; she would have accepted our proposals.

However, till the spring of 1943 they had a pleasant life. They shared two rooms with a splendid southern exposure toward the Rhine, which crossed a park in the immediate vicinity of their house. Since Jews were not allowed to buy anything friends secretly brought them wood, coal, and food. Your aunt (Granny) had an egg per day, something denied to us for years. They were also provided with reading material. Visitors regularly came to see them. Although visits to Jews were forbidden (and transgressors of the decree threatened with deportation to a camp), we went to see them several times every week and spent afternoons and evenings with them. They were *not lacking* in anything.

They were arrested, I believe in June, 1943, and imprisoned in an Arnheim school. There they were treated well; a woman friend brought them eggs and other food. Afterwards, they were taken to a camp in the Netherlands. We could still send them parcels and letters there. Then, at the beginning of the summer, they were transported to Germany . . . and then no further news. What could be done?

This very long letter from Pasteur Hayet, of the Église Wallonne d'Arnheim, was handwritten on torn paper. After telling of Granny's last days in Holland, he gave the horribly tragic story of his wife's family. Her father and his three adult sons, all Protestant ministers, were murdered in the Oranienburg concentration camp. Pasteur Hayet was later sent to such a camp himself.

These gruesome reports were followed by a plea for help. The Germans had totally ransacked his house. He needed the most necessary items for survival: sheets, toothbrushes, combs, and many other things. It was the report of a brave and honest man, who had returned from a concentration camp to find his home looted.

I am profoundly grateful that I was able to give him all the help I could. I was assisted by Allied officers at the Hilden headquarters. They could make shipments to Holland. But it was so little compared with all the kindness and help he had given to my family and to all those in the Arnheim area who had been persecuted because of their Jewishness.

———

The fine thread of hope to which I clung had not broken. This was strange, but true. The thread still held after I received the letter from Arnheim via London in July of 1945. It held until Christmas Eve of 1945.

On December 24, 1945—as a "Christmas present"— I got a letter from my sister's London solicitors:

> London, December 9, 1945
>
> With regard to Mrs. Gerta Warburg and Dr. Betty Warburg we have received confirmation that these ladies died at Sobibor on April 16, 1943.

Such news, given in black and white, is final. The thread of hope—that I would see Granny again—broke at that moment, just as the children began to sing their Christmas carols. They looked at me in astonishment. Why wasn't I singing with them?

Granny and Aunt Betty were now really dead for me.

The repaired crèche figures stretched their crippled arms toward me. I was a cripple myself. I had fallen from the height of hope. I had fallen down hard—to reality. Now my beloved ones had finally been taken from me.

In February 1947 the district office in Mettmann sent me a registered letter, asking me to pick up my denazification forms. I put this demand in a new envelope and returned it registered to the same office. I pointed out that it must be an error, because I was a persecuted person of that regime. I got another registered letter, telling me that it was *not* an error. As the manager of an enterprise that had a value above RM 100,000, I had to be denazified.

I drove to Mettmann and got the form. If it had been rolled up, it would have easily filled a roll of toilet paper. It contained 133 questions. The children stood at each side of the typewriter, helping to keep the paper straight. They thought the whole affair was rather funny. If the typewriter keys *N* and *O,* for *NO,* had been easily destructible, they would have been worn out quickly. I filled in the formula and sent the letter. Then I forgot all about it.

In August 1947 I got another registered letter: Would I please pick up my clearance papers from Mettmann and sign for them? I had been "cleared."

I refused to sign. How could I be exonerated if there had never been any charges against me?

Two years had passed. Another thread of hope had worn thinner and therefore cut into me all the more: the belief that my mother might still return.

To end my torment, I began to write and search for her systematically. I wrote to organizations that had lists of the victims murdered in concentration camps. I tried to obtain papers for declaration of death. I had to travel a sad and troublesome path. It led through Germany, Holland, and England. Finally I had all the documents. The circumstances in the case of my mother, which demonstrated the shortage of paper at that time, also took a lot out of me.

On May 7, 1948, I received the official document from the Hamburg Lower Court, with the declaration that my mother could be considered dead. This was written on a piece of old paper. The back had been used before. The old contents had been crossed out with two thick blue lines. It was a verdict from 1936. A poor person, who had embezzled RM 130.26, had been condemned to jail.

My children have never been good students. They have never liked to read books. When we were permitted to travel by car again after the war, I was planning to show them the Bavarian Baroque, a happy period of art, which I wanted them to appreciate. After I had spent three days of hard work telling my children all about it, I heard Oskar's ideas: "Please, Mum, give me a large pair of scissors. I would like to cut all church steeples out of the landscape! I can't stand a Baroque altar anymore! I am sick of all the gilded beauty!"

We drove into the Black Forest, where my children went trout fishing and swam a lot. I had learned my lesson.

As they grew older, their school reports became worse. Blue letters came in. Private tuition became necessary. I had too much work to attend to Oskar's hated Latin lessons. I thought I could impress my son by threatening him: "If you don't pull yourself together in school now and pass into the next class, I am going to put you in blue overalls and you are going to become a tradesman!"

What happened next was beyond my imagination. "How wonderful, Mum, how absolutely wonderful!" my son yelled. He caught hold of me and swung me around. "That's all I want! I would like to become a tinsmith and as soon as possible begin as an apprentice at the trailer firm in Vohwinkel!"

Oskar got into the next class. I had promised him to give in if he passed the examination. Every profession was honorable, I said, and would feed a man. What would we do without good tradesmen? I never was one for the overvaluation of intellectual professions.

Alexa did not pass her examination, which did not worry her at all. There was not a spark of school ambition in either of my children. Neither of them was interested in carrying on with either the farm or the soup industry. Until this decision of theirs, I had kept both enterprises going. Now all looked different. With my health damaged from suffering during the time of Nazi persecution, work was often hard on me, and, with the attitude of my children, it suddenly all looked rather senseless. If I had been a salaried worker, I would have been thinking about changing jobs.

Büscher took the lead in making a decision. One dark and dull autumn day he knocked at my door. He stayed near the exit and told me, with tears in his eyes, that the work was beginning to be too much for him. Now that I was over the worst, could he please leave soon, because the separation from the children and all would be very hard on him? He wanted to return to his familiar coal district. He would stay with his son and live on his pension. It certainly would not be easy for him, after all these years with me, but it just had to be that way now.

A few days later we parted, both with heavy hearts.

———

The German currency reform was over. Reichsmark 100 became Deutsche Mark 6.40, a devaluation of 93 percent. Life slowly returned to normal. Food was more plentiful and the clothing industry had started to run well. The humans began— each for himself, though—to build up again and LIVE!

Friends and acquaintances came to visit us in Gruiten and enjoyed house and garden, farm and soup industry. There was only one thing we did not agree on: my determination to let Oskar have his will and become a tinsmith. They had a fixed idea, like a mathematical formula: Two academic parents had to have a child who would at least pass his final examination. My point of view, that my children would not make it, was rejected. My friends often used the expression "inferiority complex." (How I hate this kind of expression!) They said my children would suffer from it later in life if they did not have a better education. Everybody advised me to force Oskar to go on in school.

As the only parent, not wanting to make a grave mistake, I was looking for an objective judgment. Through a friend, I sent a page from an essay book with Oskar's handwriting to a woman graphologist for the Hamburg Juvenile Court. I asked for advice on a choice of profession. No names were mentioned. The answer was short: Oskar was not suitable for an intellectual profession, but would do very well in a manual one. Optician or fine mechanic would also not be suitable.

Oskar became a tinsmith, at least for the time being.

This decision, this leaving of traditional and family ways, changed our life. I played with the idea of giving up the house and farm and emigrating with my children. My brother in South Africa offered to sponsor us. But, having been a pariah under the Nazis for so many years, I could not live in a country where I would have to bring up my children as white supremacists. I gratefully declined my brother's offer.

My sister and her second husband were willing to sponsor us in Australia. In 1950 Germans were still "enemy aliens" there. For the moment I could not decide.

―――――

In 1950 gasoline was still controlled. Rations were given out according to the importance and size of an enterprise. The coupons had to be picked up in Gruiten and signed for. I sat in one of the city hall offices, waiting for the official to return with the general ration for Gruiten. Others were also waiting. We all knew each other. We talked about this and that to shorten the waiting time.

Then the owner of a factory came in to get his ration. He asked me, "Tell me, doctor, why do you cut so much wood from your forest?"

"To make money to pay for the general war costs," I answered.

"But *you* don't pay for that, do you?"

"Certainly I pay for that also. I too, I have to pay for the lost Nazi war, only because millions of others like you wore that 'toilet lid' [*I meant the party insignia*] in their buttonholes!"

When he heard my answer, the factory owner lost his self-control. Infuriated and red in the face he exploded: "Well, doctor, now we know your attitude! Be assured that you will *not* survive the next pogrom!"

Icy, benumbed silence fell over the room. I got up and repeated the man's remark. I emphasized that I had been threatened in a public office. I asked the two lady officials if they would be witnesses in the case. They agreed. Would they kindly and as an exception send my gas coupons to my farm! I drove home.

From there I rang my lawyer in Cologne and told him what had happened. I asked him what I should do.

"Nothing," he answered. "We certainly could get a judgment against this chap, since you have two reliable witnesses, but he would not have to pay more than DM 150 [about $30], which would mean nothing to him. But *you,* you will be the cause of a lot of laughter at all Nazi meetings in the future! Take my advice: Hands off!"

I phoned the editor of the newspaper in our neighboring town. He was one of my friends, also a persecuted person. As a Jew he had been a fugitive all during the Nazi regime. I told him my story and asked him whether he could report it in his paper.

"Certainly, Tutti, if you insist," he replied, "but things like that have no importance. I can place such a story as wide as a thumb just above the advertisements, where nobody will read it, because nobody is interested in such stories."

The last decision was difficult and a profound responsibility. Three facts had to be considered: the inclination of my children for practical work only, their unwillingness to continue my work on the farm and in the factory, and my experience with further anti-Semitism in Germany, which simmered on, even after the end of the "Thousand-Year Reich."

There were two more points. The rearmament of Germany was to be expected in the near future, something I would never have thought possible in 1951. Soon Oskar would have to go the way his father did, and this for a country that had murdered at least six and a half million people, among them two of his grandparents.

Last, but not least, I had reached the maximum age at which I could still get into a foreign country, with two dependents, two children who were still minors.

The dice fell for Australia. I hoped to give my children an unburdened future in a country in which descent and tradition were unimportant. When I filled in my application form at the Australian Mission in Cologne, I realized the tremendous financial loss involved in the transfer, because at that time the German Mark was one of the weakest currencies.

On September 10, 1951, I left the country of my ancestors and drove with both my children out of the large farm gate. The red roof of the house, which had been a blessing to us and so many others, gleamed in the sun. The green of the forest, which had once been mine, stood off beautifully against a blue sky. The separation from house and estate was not difficult.

It was much harder to leave the trees I had planted twenty years ago, especially the birches, which lined the drive on both sides. I had once carried them, over my shoulder, from the forest. How tiny they were then!

On the evening before my departure I walked once more along my roses, with Granny's flat basket on my arm. Thinking of her, I had cut the faded flowers. I left the basket behind. It still belonged to Granny's Germany. And for the last time on German soil I remembered her advice:

"Stick to nature, my child. It will never hurt you!"

13

The Last Stones in the Mosaic

It is not hard to write; it reads even more easily: In October of 1951 we emigrated to Australia. But from the day we boarded an Italian migrant ship in Genoa, traveling tourist class, it was hard. For four weeks we lived in the tough conditions typical of a migrant ship. My children thought it was an adventure, but to me it seemed rather unpleasant and nerve-racking.

One should not judge the faraway Australian continent from its big cities, where most of the people live. Cities all over the world are very much alike. One should try to grasp and understand the pioneer life and the loneliness of the Australian outback. It shapes the people.

To make a clear break with the past and our own surroundings, we settled in Brisbane, the vast capital of the sunny state of Queensland. We moved into a house that was surrounded by a garden. Now fruit and flowers, which we had known in our Gruiten garden, changed into orchids and bananas, and it was good that they did.

It was easy for the children to burn their bridges behind them. They easily joined the community of their new homeland, and both finished their education with pleasure and success. They learned to esteem their countrymen. They got married in Australia and enjoy their families.

211

But for me, as a heavy-blooded North German and a tradition-minded European intellectual, it was not easy to get used to many Queensland ways, which seemed rather Victorian to me. I finally learned to value all the people I had to deal with. In a sense, I stepped back into the horse-and-buggy days, when life in Australia was hard. Farms were then very far apart and could be reached only on horseback. I found hospitality and a helping hand all over the country.

Twelve years in Australia, from 1951 to 1963, taught me how difficult it is for a widow to earn the money to feed three people in a strange country and to educate two children as well. I had given myself the task of merging a bit of European culture and civilization with the life style of this far-away Continent. I intended to bring understanding to the people and I wanted to serve the cause of peace. I had seen enough unrest and war. I feel that I managed this self-appointed goal as a lecturer for adult education in Queensland. This job took me to the distant parts of this large Australian state.

I returned to Europe in 1957 to photograph and collect material for lectures. During this stay I visited some of Granny's relatives in Holland. The husband had gotten his bank training in Hamburg in the twenties and had often been Granny's guest in the Hochallee. As a Jew, he had had to wear the Yellow Star in Nazi-occupied Holland. Because he had married an "Aryan," he was not sent to a camp, but had to report to the SA every day.

But his old mother and his brother, who suffered from multiple sclerosis and who was slightly disturbed mentally, had been sent to the Westerbork camp, where Granny and Aunt Betty had been sent after their stay in Arnheim. With tears in her eyes the "Aryan" wife of our relative told me about her last meeting with my family. It was during one of her visits to Westerbork. The surgeon Dr. med. Betty Warburg had offered her some poison for her sick brother-in-law, so that he could be saved from Nazi torture. They would have enough for themselves. Hoping that her brother-in-law would survive, the woman rejected the kind offer. She did not want a murder on her conscience, she told my people.

So by sheer coincidence I learned that Granny and Aunt Betty had had enough poison to end their lives themselves.

With this knowledge, although the horror remained, in 1957 I returned to Brisbane, to my children and to my work.

As the years passed, I discovered that my health, which had suffered during my Nazi persecution, had gotten much worse in the hot subtropical climate. I was often very sick indeed, and no medical help could be given. But as long as my children were not fully assimilated, there was no possibility of returning to Europe and a milder climate. Only after 1963, when my children had finished their education and gotten married, did I dare to take the last step: I separated—as hard as it was—from children and grandchildren and returned to the European world, where I belonged. My heart was full of gratitude to Australia, which had done so much for my children and me.

But I also thank Switzerland every day, for permission to live in a forlorn little Tessin village. In this climate I feel much better.

It was here that in 1964 I got a letter from my former Amsterdam notary, with whom I had fought for Granny's restitution. He told me that there was still a case of restitution of jewelry to be settled with the German government. My first reaction was: For God's sake, don't start again. Leave me in peace away from all those gruesome happenings!

But, because I was in Holland at that time, I went to see the notary. It was a very moving meeting, because for years we had exchanged letters without ever having met. A thick folder represented our former work.

The notary told me that there was a Jewish organization in Holland. It was very honorable and worked correctly, but it was tough. Recently they had gotten lists of all the people killed in the Sobibor death camp. The lists also contained the names of all people from whom jewelry had been taken before they were killed by gas. The names of Gerta and Betty Warburg were mentioned in these lists. As the facts showed, three golden watches had been taken from these ladies.

The lists had been made with German tidiness and accuracy and had been put in a safe place. They had now come into the hands of the organization the notary had told me about. As trustee for the Burchard heirs, I was asked for my signature so that the matter could be pursued. I hesitated to sign. It all was too gruesome! I was told that I did not have to give anything away and that other members of the family might ask me for an explanation of my refusal. I signed.

To regain my self-control, I went into the Rijksmuseum. For a long, long time I admired one of the tenderest paintings in this world. I sat quietly before Rembrandt's "The Jewish Bride."

In 1964, I got the gruesome, written certainty that, in the Sobibor death camp, the Germans had taken three golden watches from my people. This meant that the poison, of which the Dutch lady had spoken in 1957, had no longer been in their possession and that they could not have ended their lives themselves. To me it was now certain that Granny, my Granny, nearly blind and eighty-six years old, had been sent to Sobibor and that she and her daughter Betty had had to drink their goblet to the dregs. . . .

The descendants of Albert and Gerta Warburg have been scattered over the countries of this earth, the same as the remains of the murdered dead ones. No old tombstone will survive to remind later generations of the past.

With astonishment I look into the faces of my children and grandchildren, searching for a resemblance to Granny. I do not find it.

APPENDIX

About the Nazi Death Camp Sobibor

The following data were contained in an article from the Dutch press, July 9, 1947:

From March 2, 1942, to July 20, 1943, 34,313 Jews were gassed in Sobibor. A Red Cross report notes that during that period, week after week, one train went to the KZ Sobibor. All in all, only 19 persons, 16 women and 3 men, returned. As for the rest, all persons younger than 17 or older than 35 years of age must be assumed to have perished. The day of their arrival may be considered as their day of death.

Since 1943, Sobibor was, according to the Red Cross, the camp of destruction for all Jews deported from Holland. It was located about 80 km to the east of Lublin, near the Russian-German line of demarcation. Sobibor was not a labor camp. It was set up in 1941. Already before the beginning of 1943 tens of thousands of Polish, Russian and Austrian Jews had been gassed there. It was a specifically Jewish camp, whose gas chambers could take about 600 people. The gas was channeled into the chamber by douches. Once the people had died, the floor turned and their remains dropped. The suitcases of the dead people were sorted and their contents shipped to Germany.

No selection process took place. The arrivals were gassed almost without exception. From a few transports, young women and men were selected for labor. Some of them were put to work exclusively in connection with the gassings. Others were sent at once to nearby camps in the District of Lublin. A so-called children's transport (consisting only of children with their mothers) arrived at Sobibor from Vught via Westerbork and was gassed immediately upon arrival—with no survivors.

On November 8, 1943, the Germans carried out their radical plan of destruction in all Jewish camps and ghettos in the District of Lublin. The entire camp of Sobibor and all other camps nearby and in the entire District of Lublin were liquidated. This included people who had not been gassed immediately upon arrival; they, too, died before November 8, 1943. With the exception of the 19 people mentioned, nobody returned.

(Details about the KZ Sobibor were related to the German people in 1966 during the trial at Hagen, Westphalia, against some of the assassins).

As reported by well-informed people, between 500,000 and 600,000 persons were murdered at Sobibor.